Developing Skills for Community Care

A collaborative approach

Peter Beresford
Steve Trevillion

arena

Published by
Arena
Ashgate Publishing Limited
Gower House
Croft Road
Aldershot
Hants GU11 3HR
England

Ashgate Publishing Company
Old Post Road
Brookfield
Vermont 05036
USA

British Library Cataloguing in Publication Data

Beresford, Peter
  Developing Skills for Community Care:
  Collaborative Approach
  I. Title   II. Trevillion, Steve
  361.941

Library of Congress Catalog Card Number: 94-80265

ISBN 1 85742 237 6 (paperback)
ISBN 1 85742 236 8 (hardback)

Typeset by Manton Typesetters, 5–7 Eastfield Road, Louth, Lincolnshire LN11 7AJ.
Printed in Great Britain by Hartnoll's Ltd, Bodmin

Contents

Foreword

Radical leaps in social policy such as the one we have recently gone through always produce banner statements. The words 'collaboration', 'empowerment' and 'participation' leap from the mouths of speakers and from the pages of books and articles. An important first stage, but also one of danger. Good intentions can be wrecked by assumptions about agreement where there is none, and a failure to work on what must underpin intentions. This is particularly important in social care where practice is about the day-to-day detail and diversity of people's lives. Generalizations are not only inadequate, they are oppressive. An essential second stage is moving towards greater clarity about banner headlines, including differences of interpretation, and the sort of practice which is most likely to bring us closest to achieving change.

This book makes an important contribution to remedying the neglect of the development of practice at a time when the initial concentration on implementation has been concerned with organizational structures and procedures. The book is based on working with managers, practitioners, service users and carers, drawing on their experience to identify the skills and approaches needed for community care. Using a 'bottom up' approach, the authors have been able to model their own views about the importance of collaboration. Although they argue major changes are needed, there are existing resources which can be built on. Peter Beresford and Steve Trevillion make a strong case for giving a greater emphasis to skills such as negotiation, networking and information-giving, but they equally stress the importance of traditional ones, like relationship-building and communication.

Creating collaborative practice in social care will be achieved only through doing, analysing and disseminating research in a form which is useful to managers, practitioners, service users and carers. It will not emerge of itself. *Developing Skills for Community Care* combines these merits with being easy to read and to use. Thank you Peter and Steve and all those who worked with you.

Daphne Statham, Director, National Institute for Social Work

Acknowledgements

We have many people to thank for making this book possible. We particularly want to thank the service users and carers and their organizations who took part in the project. We would also like to thank the nurses, social workers and managers who took part. We owe special thanks to Steve Cribb, Millie Brister, Brian Spencer, Cherna Crome, Sheila Caiden and Cilla Ankrah-Lucas for their help in setting up discussions with service users and carers, to Tessa Harding and Hardeesh Rai for their help in networking and to Mandy Batra, Sukhvir Bansal and Angela Kainth for their help in enabling the involvement of Asian women.

We would like to thank Betula Nelson and Naseem Shah of West London Institute and Suzy Croft of Open Services Project for all their help, especially during the groupwork phase of the development project, which we would not have been able to manage on our own. Malcolm Fyfe of Hounslow Social Services and Dipak Shah of Camden Social Services provided continuous support and encouragement, and we are pleased to have this opportunity to recognize the key role that they played in enabling us to undertake the project. Thanks go to Suki Montford and Catherine Beresford for their help. We are grateful to the Central Council for Education and Training in Social Work for funding the development project upon which the book is based and Jo Gooderham of Arena for her encouragement and commitment to the book.

Finally, we would like to say thank you to Fenella, Rachel and Phillip, for coping so well with the way in which the process of writing this book disrupted their lives, and to Ruth, whose requests to 'play bricks', 'watch telly' and 'talk me' provided some welcome interruptions.

Introduction

The challenge of change

Massive changes in welfare generally and community care specifically are now taking place. These are making enormous demands for innovation and change on human service workers. The aim of this book is to help service workers make this move successfully. It seeks to do this by setting out a new collaborative approach for practice, consistent with the new values and goals of needs-led service and user involvement. The model of practice developed in this book is based on the practical experience, insights and proposals of service users, carers and practitioners.

The changes now taking place in welfare and community care are far-reaching. They include new welfare philosophy and legislation, changed structures and organizations and new theories developed by disabled people and service users. In Britain, health, local authorities and personal social services are all undergoing reorganization. There are new community care cultures, language and roles, all requiring new skills.

How will workers negotiate all this, so that, in the words of one of the service users we spoke to, they are still in a position to help the service users they are working with? So far radical change has not been accompanied by the development of the radically different model of practice which it requires. Instead the response has often been to retreat to the past rather than to look to the future.

A new approach to practice

We hope this book will help change this. We believe that the collaborative approach to practice it discusses does not just offer another way of delivering traditional welfare services, but instead is a way of transforming the nature of welfare systems. It offers an alternative to the paternalism of the old state services and the new competitiveness of the market.

Collaboration is not a new idea. It is meant to be one of the foundations of the new community care. But it is one thing to make a rhetorical commitment to collaboration, another to make it a practical reality. The aim of this book is to provide agencies and practitioners with a basis for doing so.

While it does not duck theoretical, philosophical or value issues, the book is rooted in service users', carers' and practitioners' day-to-day experience. It develops practice from the bottom up, not from the top down. The book draws on a development project which involved service users, carers and practitioners in exploring and negotiating the skills needed for community care. The project was itself an exercise in collaboration and it demonstrated that a collaborative approach could work. This book seeks to communicate the lessons learned from both the findings and the process of the project.

Breaking down barriers

Perhaps the most exciting lesson we learned from the development project was that there *was* a way forward. Service users, carers and practitioners could work together and they could find common ground about skills for community care. No less important, the model of practice which grew out of their collaboration took into account the reality of limited resources, instead of ignoring it or being undermined by it.

This book has been written for human service practitioners who want to work in more equal and participatory ways. Its overall aim is to help workers support service users to have the opportunities, rights, choices and support which they want in their lives. It is for people who want to develop more collaborative ways of working with colleagues, both within and outside their own agencies, as well as with service users and carers and their organizations. The book provides guidelines, checklists and exercises based on the development project to help readers to monitor and develop their collaborative practice.

This book challenges many of the barriers that exist in community care. It connects the different world-views of service users, carers and practitioners and reveals the important areas of agreement between them. It shows that inter-agency collaboration and user involvement, which have tended to be treated separately, are actually closely connected and entail comparable skills. It makes connections between user involvement, anti-oppression and anti-discriminatory working. It shows the overlaps between different professions and highlights the need to start from a notion of community care practice instead of from traditional professional disciplines. Above all the book, like the practice approach it advocates, rests on the belief that welfare and community care policy and services are likely to be most supportive and most cost-effective if all the key constituencies concerned – practitioners, service users, carers, and other local people – are fully and equally involved in shaping and controlling them.

The structure of the book

Now let's turn to the structure of the book. At the end of each chapter, readers will find a short summary of its discussion.

Chapter One focuses on collaboration. It examines the new emphasis on collaboration in community care and points out some of the problems in moving from rhetoric to reality. We see how collaboration unifies two key requirements in community care: cooperation between professions and the involvement of service users. We begin the process of defining collaboration and look at what collaboration may and may not mean in practice.

Chapter Two moves on to the development project on which the book is based. The aim of the project was to identify a core of skills associated with a collaborative approach to community care, in response to the growing recognition of the importance of training for collaboration in community care. The project was itself an exercise in collaboration, involving service users, carers and community care practitioners. Two ideas central to collaboration in community care are discussed – networking and user involvement – and the thinking which underpinned the project is also examined.

Chapter Three begins to look at what practitioners and managers in the development project had to say about community care skills. It explains how they were involved in the project and examines the first stage of this process, the community care diaries they kept of their day-to-day practice. Analysis of this shows a strong link between a needs-led and collaborative approach to practice, highlighting the factors which encourage collaborative practice as well as some of its characteristics.

Chapter Four reports on the discussions with practitioners about their practice. It examines a range of themes which emerged from these discussions about collaborative skills and explores their relationship with a collaborative culture. These include the management of conflict, resources, power sharing, support, the organizational context, building networks and training.

Chapter Five turns to the discussions with service users and carers. It describes the process by which they were involved in the project and then reports each group's experience of and attitudes to community care and the skills they identify for community care. It also focuses on their views of the range of skills required for collaboration by *both* practitioners and service users and carers.

Chapter Six moves on to a series of broader issues about collaboration and community care skills which service users and carers raised in the project. These related both to themselves and to service agencies and practitioners. They include differences between health and social services, the interrelation of skills and values, ensuring services are equally accessible to all communities, service users' and carers' own training needs and the implications of people having different levels of experience and involvement in community care. In the second part of the chapter a series of guidelines for involving service users and carers are offered, based on the experience of the project.

Chapter Seven looks at the final stage of the development project, the meeting which brought together service users, carers and practitioners and enabled each group first to explore its own views on skills and collaboration for community care and then to come together to exchange them with the others. It reports the set of skills which the three groups were jointly able to identify and prioritize and examines the process for the meeting which made this collaboration possible.

Chapter Eight looks at what we have learned about collaboration so far. Building on the development project, it sets out the defining characteristics of a collaboration culture and looks at how to develop one and what is needed for it to flourish. It offers a series of guidelines or checklists of the basics for practitioners who want to work more collaboratively. These basics include credibility, anti-oppressive values and empowerment. Then it looks at some of the training implications and offers a self-evaluation exercise for readers to check and develop their own basic skills in collaborative work.

Chapter Nine moves on from the basics to ideas for building a collaborative culture and examines the key skills needed to do this, including both interpersonal and inter-organizational skills. A set of exercises are provided for readers to test and develop their own collaborative skills. These include skills in communication, relationship work, empowerment, assessment and planning, collaborative working, and review and evaluation.

Finally, in a short **Conclusion**, we try to pull together the discussion about collaboration in community care and highlight some of the key themes which have emerged in this book.

1 Collaboration in community care

A cultural revolution

The new rationale of community care in Britain puts the service user centre stage. For the first time, it explicitly states that it is the needs of service users, not of services, agencies, authorities or professionals, which should guide policy and practice. Service users and carers know that this is a promise rather than a cast-iron guarantee, but even so it still represents a fundamental change in human services, with potentially far-reaching consequences.

To make services more responsive in this way to the needs and wishes of those who use them will involve the development of a radical alternative to the traditional service-led culture which has dominated all aspects of the welfare state since its inception. In the words of the Social Services Inspectorate, who have in recent years played a major part in the implementation of government policy:

> This will entail a progressive revision of organisational structures and procedures, but above all, a change in attitude and approach by managers and practitioners at every level that amounts to creating a new organisational culture (Department of Health, Social Services Inspectorate, 1991, p. 11).

So community care represents a cultural revolution. But what kind of cultural revolution? What is this new 'needs-led' culture that everyone seems to be talking about?

That there is more than one answer to this question is a direct consequence of the fact that community care itself is associated with at least two very different visions of need and the process of meeting need. These are a *market* and a *collaboration* vision. We need to look at them both before we go any further.

5

Meeting need through the market

This vision is based on an image of the service user as a consumer whose needs can be neatly quantified and then met through a flourishing care market. Services are assumed to be needs-led because competition is supposed to ensure 'the customer is king'. This has been described as 'supermarket style consumerism' (Walker, 1993, p. 221).

Whether service users can ever be 'customers' in the true sense of the word is a much debated point, especially when there are few examples of these so-called customers actually purchasing services (Morris, 1993). But few would argue that 'contract culture' has not made a major impact on the way in which services are designed, purchased and packaged, which could be described as revolutionary (Hoyes and Means, 1993, p. 290).

Meeting need through collaboration

The collaborative vision of a needs-led or user-led community care system is one in which power is shifted from professionals to communities, service users and carers. It is one in which needs are identified through discussion, support mobilized through negotiation and a wide range of practitioners cooperate with one another across both traditional organizational boundaries and the new boundaries between purchasers and providers.

But, while market principles have become an increasingly influential part of the post-welfare state world, it is by no means clear that there has been a parallel collaborative revolution. On the face of it, this is puzzling. The involvement of service users and carers and the achievement of 'seamless' patterns of inter-agency and inter-professional work are explicit policy objectives (Department of Health, Social Services Inspectorate, 1991, pp. 2–3).

It may be simply that it takes time for people and organizations to change their ways. But it is also true that it seems to be much easier to encourage purchasers and providers to compete with one another than to cooperate with one another and involve service users and carers in key decisions. After all, competition allows community care organizations and individual practitioners to exercise a new kind of market power whereas collaboration requires that they share power both with one another and with service users and carers.

But even if we make the assumption that practitioners want to cooperate with one another, it is now clear that as the community care service environment has become more and more competitive, so it has become increasingly difficult for people to trust one another or to spend time (and therefore money!) developing collaborative relationships.

Another problem is the sheer complexity of the issues which seem to be raised by any attempt to move from rhetoric about collaboration to anything that might resemble collaborative practice. There are so many different individuals, organizations and professional interests involved, so many different perceptions of need and so many different priorities, that it may sometimes seem as if community care is a hopelessly tangled knot which will never be unravelled.

Even the government, while exhorting all those involved to collaborate effectively, has not been able to conceal the apparently daunting scale of the task. Quite apart from service users and carers who are themselves distinct if overlapping groups, there are many professions and agencies which it has specifically identified as needing to work together, such as:

> Social workers, G.P's, community nurses, hospital staff such as consultants in geriatric medicine, psychiatry, rehabilitation and other hospital specialities, nurses, physiotherapists, occupational therapists, speech therapists, continence advisors, community psychiatric nurses, staff involved with vision and hearing impairments, housing officers, the Employment Department's Resettlement Officers and its Employment Rehabilitation Service, home helps, home care assistants and voluntary workers (Cmn 849, 1989, p. 19, s.3.2.5).

But before this apparent complexity leads us to dismiss the whole venture of collaboration as misconceived, we should consider the possibility that what may be making the problem so apparently insoluble is our way of looking at it.

A new approach

Conventionally, the involvement of service users and carers has been discussed as if it had little connection with the ability of practitioners to 'work effectively together' (Griffiths, 1988, p. 14, s.6.4; Cmn 849, 1989, pp. 13, s.2.20 and 19, s.3.2.6).

Only now have we begun to grasp what should perhaps have been obvious from the beginning. Collaboration with service users and carers, and collaboration between different groups of practitioners, should not be treated as two separate issues, but as part of a *single* transformation of the whole way in which we think about what has come to be known as community care. This is the cultural revolution for which we are still waiting.

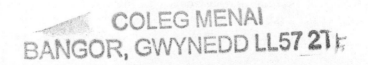

Community care and independent living

During the forty or so years that the term 'community care' has been in existence, a number of different meanings have been attached to it. Initially it was used to mean moving people from large to smaller institutions: from hospitals, former workhouses and prisons to hostels and homes. Now it is also used to mean supporting people so they can stay in their own homes, and supported schemes to enable people to live in ordinary housing, as well as small-scale group living.

Disabled people and other service users increasingly challenge the idea of community care – a combination of two of the most contested, ill-defined and devalued words in the language. Shortly we shall see how many service users are critical of the concept of 'care' in public provision. For such service users the concept of community care is associated with inferior and controlling provision which is part of a segregated welfare system.

Rejecting this, some disabled people have developed instead the idea of *independent living*. It is helpful first to look more carefully at the word independent. Disabled people argue that in welfare services independent has usually been taken to mean people being able to do things for themselves and to live without support. They have therefore been defined as dependent because of their need for support: for example, to get up, dress, eat and get about.

Disabled people's concept of independence is related to the social model of disability which they have developed. This rejects an individual or medical model of disability, which sees the major cause of people's disability as their impairment, and instead highlights the disabling effects of societies which discriminate against and exclude people with physical, mental and sensory impairments.

Disabled people have redefined independence. They argue that it should mean having the support to ensure the rights, choices and opportunities available to non-disabled people, thus making access possible to employment, recreation, public transport, the environment and so on. So, for example, they say:

> Here the term 'independent' does not refer to someone who can do everything themselves, a feat that no human being can achieve, whether they have an impairment or not, but indicates someone who is able to take control of their own life and to choose how that life should be led … Independent living … is primarily about giving disabled people access to and control of a range of community based services which enable them to identify and pursue their own lifestyle (Barnes, 1991, pp. 129–30).

Disabled people argue that independence should be measured not by the physical tasks that disabled people can or cannot perform, but rather by the personal and economic decisions that they can make. Thus independent living means access to the support which enables each individual to live as they want to, and the same access to employment, housing, income, education and other services, rights and responsibilities as the rest of the population. Such a definition of independence does not deny people's interdependence. Independent living becomes the goal of user-led services.

The concept of independent living enables us to escape – at least in our imaginations – from the closed universe of 'care givers' and 'care receivers'. In a world in which choices become real and needs are defined in ways which suit individuals rather than welfare agencies, it is no longer possible for professionals to refuse to talk to one another or to fail to respond to service users and carers. Enabling independence is not about promoting self-sufficiency, it is about the process of developing flexible and user-driven networks of support – a process we would describe as collaboration.

To initiate this process, often little more is required than paying attention to what service users are actually saying. What emerges is often something very simple but, at the same time, far-reaching in its implications. This, for example, is what some black disabled people want:

> The concept of Community Care will not be different for Black Disabled people. The principles of choice and independence are valued as much by Black Disabled people as they are by others. However, policy makers and practitioners must acknowledge and work with the fact that Black Disabled people need support to enable them to achieve autonomy and a lifestyle which they value as Black Disabled people (Begum, 1994, p. 144).

This challenges traditional, sometimes racist, community care practices. But it also clearly indicates a way forward for all concerned. Professional rivalries and organizational conflicts and misunderstandings do not disappear overnight. But a shared commitment to the key principles of 'choice' and 'independence' and a shared understanding of the key task of enabling black disabled (and other) people to obtain the support they want establishes a common framework and helps to put these problems into perspective.

Empowerment

It should be clear by now that we see collaboration as an empowering strategy.

There has been an enormous increase in interest in the idea of empowerment in both community care and human services more generally. Empowerment is now officially identified as a central function of community care, as well as the purpose of professional practice. However, there is little clarity or agreement about the meaning of empowerment. Service users' definitions of empowerment tend to follow on from their strong sense of *disempowerment*. They experience oppression, discrimination and restrictions on their rights, opportunities and choices. Empowerment for them means reversing this situation. So for example:

> Being empowered means having control over my life and being able to influence others. It means opportunities for people to influence the system collectively, to have control over our own lives (Evans, 1994).

This approach to empowerment is concerned with changing people's position in society. It does not ignore issues of personal empowerment, but these are framed in terms of ensuring people the support, skills and personal resources they need both to organize themselves and to participate to achieve broader social and political change.

Professional interest in empowerment is generally more narrowly concerned with personal empowerment: with people taking increased responsibility for managing their lives, relationships and circumstances in order to live in conformity with prevailing values and expectations and to change in accordance with professionally set goals and norms. This has led one commentator to suggest that the professional approach to empowerment has important regulatory as well as liberatory implications (Baistow, 1995).

Some service users reject the idea that professionals can empower them, arguing that 'we can only empower ourselves'. This is not a view we share. We believe workers can help service users develop personal empowerment by providing information and increasing people's expectations, assertiveness and self-esteem. They can also give people access to resources, opportunities, networks and organizations. In this way they can provide a helpful basis for service users to gain more say and control. But service users' and professionals' interpretations of empowerment may be different. This highlights the need for clarity when talking about empowerment and when using it as a guiding principle for working together.

Working together – rhetoric and reality

Unfortunately, empowerment is not the only word we need to be cautious about.

The popularity of certain other 'buzz words' can also be a problem. For example, the temptation for practitioners to describe any service users or carers with whom they are in contact as 'partners' may be irresistible. This desire for 'partnership' may be quite genuine. But good intentions are not enough and the ease with which it is possible to use fashionable terminology may distract us from the messy and complex business of attempting to build genuinely collaborative relationships with service users and carers.

Likewise, with inter-professional or inter-agency 'partnerships'. There is so much emphasis on concepts such as 'the multi-disciplinary team' and 'teamwork in primary care' (Thomas and Corney, 1993, pp. 47–48) that professionals seem to feel obliged to use the language of partnership almost indiscriminately. This point was brought home to us at the very beginning of the project on which this book is based.

In response to questions about collaboration, many of those who took part – both social workers and nurses – tended at first to list all those professionals with whom they had some kind of regular contact as 'partners'.

In the context of collaboration, language is plainly even more slippery than usual. We therefore need to be clear about the words we are using and why we are using them.

Partnership and collaboration

Partnership is rooted in the concept of participation. When the social work profession gave 'client participation' a central place in its code of ethics (British Association of Social Workers, 1980), an important shift was made away from the notion of the 'client' or 'patient' as a passive recipient of services. Since then, concepts of partnership have been extended to include both relationships between practitioners and carers/families and the way in which practitioners relate to one another, that is to say, those issues which have often been separately described as 'multi-disciplinary teamwork' and 'inter-agency work' (see Trevillion, 1992, for a discussion about communities and partnership).

However, it has become increasingly clear that when it comes to trying to understand the ways in which practitioners relate to one another and to service users and carers on a day-to-day basis, the concept of partnership is not always helpful. This is partly because almost everyone seem to have their own ideas about what it means. It also needs to be said that for many service users and carers, the concept of partnership comes dragging with it a deadweight of disappointment, false expectations and denial because of the failure of those who promoted it most avidly to take sufficient account of conflict and inequalities of power and control (Morris, 1993). While not denying that it has some value under some circumstances, we will in this book make more use of the term 'collaboration' to refer to the various forms of working together.

Anxieties about identity

It has to be acknowledged that like empowerment and partnership the term collaboration is not without its problems. For many people it evokes the concept of 'betrayal'. But in making explicit a fear which we all have about selling out as the price of a closer relationship with those we have tradition-ally kept at arm's length, this image of collaboration as betrayal may actu-ally help us to confront our anxieties and force us to separate fantasy from reality.

There may be times when we should refuse to collaborate if we feel that what is being asked of us is to forget who we are or to forgo our own legitimate interests and concerns. Of course, it takes courage to take a principled stand against this kind of collaboration. But on other occasions, even more courage may be required to do something to end the trench warfare which is sadly all too characteristic of relationships in the field of community care.

Furthermore, collaboration need not be an all-or-nothing exercise. In co-operating with others, we do not necessarily lose our own identity or val-ues, any more than we necessarily safeguard our identity or values by refusing to have any contact with them.

Those, for example, in the social work profession who have responded to the challenge of community care by arguing for a return to a purer form of traditional social casework seem to us not only to be falsifying the history of the profession but to be, in effect, advocating a retreat from any active engagement with the contemporary realities of welfare.

To practitioners concerned about losing their identity in the collaborative process, we would say that the real choice is between courting irrelevance by seeking to protect an idealized image of the past or developing a new and more appropriate professional identity by accepting the reality of change and engaging with it in a positive and principled way.

Is collaboration just common sense?

While accepting that collaboration is important, it could be argued that it is just common sense – people learning how to get on together, hardly some-thing which one needs to write a book about. But it is precisely this common-sense view about collaboration which needs to be challenged, because it prevents us from asking the questions we need to ask. We can illustrate this by looking at three 'common-sense' notions about collaboration which are in fact very misleading, because although they all begin by stating an obvious truth, they go on to draw misleading conclusions.

Collaboration is working closely with somebody else (Rao, 1991, p. 14).

[Therefore, anybody with whom we work closely must be someone with whom we are collaborating.]

Is this really so? What about members of the same team? Or the relationship between supervisors and those they supervise? Both involve close working relationships but neither is necessarily an example of collaboration. Collaboration has to involve something more than simply working closely with other people, otherwise it becomes so broad as to be meaningless.

Collaboration involves having a good relationship with other people with whom one is working (Rao, 1991, p. 31).

[Therefore, those whom one feels closest to, like most or have the least conflict with are those with whom one is collaborating.]

This is not always true. A good relationship, if this is defined as a trouble-free relationship, may be a product of *not* working closely together rather than doing so. Moreover, a difficult relationship may be difficult precisely because those involved are trying to work through conflict in the spirit of collaboration rather than trying to ignore it (Payne, 1993, p. 49). Collaboration often involves taking the risk of having some conflict in order to build a meaningful working relationship.

Collaboration is based on a perception of common interest (Trevillion, 1992, pp. 22–37).

[Therefore, the concept of collaboration applies only to relationships between those whose interests are identical.]

This is a distortion of the true picture. While a perception of common interest plays an important part in collaboration, that does not mean that we should assume a complete convergence of interest. Ask yourself, are your interests the same as those of all the carers and service users you know? Are they the same as those of the other professionals you work closely with? In many ways, it is the need to negotiate different interests which is the hallmark of the *collaborative process*.

While recognizing that the concept of collaboration may necessarily be somewhat fuzzy at the edges, these examples show that we need a definition of collaboration and one which is strong enough to take account of the issues that have just been raised.

Definitions

If we turn to the dictionary for help we find that 'collaboration' is usually associated with:

a process by which two or more persons 'unite' or 'come together'

and

a shared task or purpose (Oxford English Dictionary).

It is not simply friendship or general socializing. Collaboration is a process of 'working together' and, as it involves shared aims and goals, all those involved in collaboration presumably must have an opportunity to help define those aims and goals. Moreover, the fact that the task is a shared one implies that those involved need to work together. In other words, there must be a collaborative task if there is to be a collaborative process.

The dictionary also helps us to distinguish between collaboration and total amalgamation. Collaboration is not about 'combining into one uniform whole' (Oxford English Dictionary) but about the coming together of a number of *different* individuals or groups for a *specific* set of purposes.

This notion of a level of difference which is never entirely lost, however deep or lengthy the collaboration, means that collaboration is always, at least in principle, *reversible*. Those who collaborate retain their own separate identity while simultaneously demonstrating a commitment to one another. The test of this is something we know only too well. Those who collaborate at one point may cease to collaborate at another! The process of collaboration can never be taken for granted.

To sum up:

Collaboration involves different individuals, groups or agencies working together towards agreed aims and goals on matters of mutual interest and concern by effectively and equitably deploying their collective resources.

What this definition shows is that where collaboration exists, the advantages are obvious. What it does not reveal is that the process of developing collaboration is by no means straightforward.

Collaboration involves sharing power and negotiating issues connected with different perceptions, values and interests so as to promote the collective ability to work together.

This suggests that it is by looking at the collaborative process that we will begin to see why collaboration poses such a radical challenge to traditional ways of working and amounts to a new kind of culture.

The culture of collaboration: a creative paradox

One way of thinking about the culture of collaboration is as a set of 'basic assumptions' (Schein, 1985, p. 6), simultaneously motivating those involved in collaborative work and helping them to to make sense of the processes in which they are engaged (Pedison and Sorenson, 1989, p. 2).

Always and everywhere the mainspring of collaborative culture is a paradox – respect for *difference* and commitment to *collective* action. The creativity of the collaboration will often spring from the tension between the idea that 'the whole is greater than the sum of its parts' and the principle that differences must be acknowledged and valued. The strength or otherwise of a collaborative culture is likely to reflect the extent to which this paradox is resolved.

But developing a collaborative culture cannot be achieved simply by redesignating social workers and nurses as 'care managers' or by reorganizing social services departments and health authorities. It involves a distinctive kind of approach to the way in which community care should be defined and delivered.

In the following sections we compare and contrast collaboration with other models of welfare and explore the implications for community care.

From collectivism to collective action

Traditional collectivism draws its inspiration from the belief that the state can act as the embodiment of the community and overcome the competitive and overly individualized features of contemporary society.

But although collectivism starts with the desire to rebuild relationships shattered by the development of individualism, experience suggests that it is led by its own logic to take power away from individuals and give it to the state. Cooperation and collaboration then become little more than *metaphors* vaguely connecting the organizations of the welfare state to the *ideal* of community. State welfare is not incompatible with the principle of collaboration, but does not in itself guarantee that the planning and delivery of services is characterized by either shared aims or joint patterns of working. Indeed it has been argued that the lack of this kind of reciprocity is one of the defining features of state welfare organizations (Benn, 1982, p. 52).

As far as the UK is concerned, the irony is that in attempting to recreate the community through the medium of state bureaucracy, collectivism did little or nothing either to address the problems of confusion and fragmentation characteristic of welfare services themselves or to overcome the alienation of the users of services from that which was offered to them in the name of the community.

Collectivism fails to deliver a genuinely collaborative form of welfare provision because it fails to recognize that, while the state may represent 'the community' at a symbolic level, it is, at a practical level, organized around the same principles of hierarchy and division of labour which it is expected to overcome.

Collaboration in any meaningful sense has to be based upon more than an attempt to bureaucratize and standardize in the name of the community. It has to be founded on an acknowledgement of, and a respect for, the differences that characterize every facet of society and the welfare systems that have been set up to meet its needs. From this perspective, the challenge of community care is to find ways of doing this which also enable all those involved to work together on the planning, purchasing and delivery of services. In other words, it involves a shift from collectivism in which the state acts for the community to a more direct form of collective action, one which recognizes differences as well as commonalities.

Collaboration as a principle of community care involves a fundamental reorientation in thinking about the relationship between welfare and community, from a set of services offered by the state on behalf of the community to a process of building support in which all those involved come together to define needs and to contribute collectively to the meeting of them. The role of the state continues to be associated with the principle of equity, but this objective is no longer identified with the bureaucratization and standardization of services.

From contract culture to collaboration culture

Competition creates a zero sum game in which there are always losers as well as winners. Even if there is cooperation, it is in the form of a business contract – a short-term arrangement under the terms of which both partners gain. Here the relationship counts for nothing and indeed represents nothing other than mutual self-interest (Benn, 1982, p. 45). Community care has encouraged the growth both of competition and of precisely this kind of contracting process – an approach to health and social welfare which is often referred to as 'contract culture'. This has little in common with what we would like to call 'collaboration culture'. We have no wish to introduce any additional jargon into a field which already has more than enough of it; however, it seems to us that collaboration is as much a culture as it is an activity and that linking the two words together in this way serves an important purpose.

What distinguishes collaboration culture from contract culture?

Collaboration culture values complexity, celebrates difference and yet retains a belief in the importance of power sharing and the need to develop a shared vision of both ends and means. In a collaboration culture there is a strong emphasis on collective action – something which is entirely absent from, even contrary to, the spirit of contract culture. One of the main effects of the introduction of market principles into welfare has been increasingly to fragment services and make planning and collective action more, rather than less difficult (Challis, 1990, pp. 65–85). It does not seem likely that the disintegrative power of the market can be transformed into an integrative mechanism just by redesignating it as a quasi-market (Le Grand, 1990). Markets may bring all kinds of benefits but collective action is unlikely to be one of them.

And yet we cannot leave the debate there. In the same way that the state continues to fulfil an essential though somewhat changed role in a collaborative context, so too the market will clearly form part of the welfare landscape in which the new culture of collaboration will be built.

We do not pretend to have a full answer to the question of how to reconcile two such very different principles. At a practical level, one obvious way of beginning to do so is to identify and acknowledge any conflicts of market interest at the early stages of any collaborative venture. But perhaps we should not assume too readily that collaboration and competition are always and everywhere opposed to one another. The presence of market elements, while certainly acting as a constraint upon collaboration In some areas, should not be seen as making it impossible to achieve in others. It may be that competition will increasingly create a need for collaboration. This may not be as contradictory as it sounds.

By making competition manageable, collaboration will increasingly provide an essential framework of predictability within the market which might be of mutual benefit to all those involved in it. There is some evidence that this is precisely what happens in the commercial sector itself (Alter and Hage, 1993, pp. 44–80). It may not be too far-fetched to suggest that in the field of community care the development of such networks may eventually start to have an impact on the nature of the market itself, but with what results we cannot at present tell.

To sum up, while collaboration is philosophically distinct from collectivism and competition, it is compatible with a continuing role for both the state and the market in social welfare.

Collaboration and managerialism

Collaboration culture may be compatible with both markets and the concept of state welfare, but is it compatible with being part of an organization, particularly in an era of what has come to be known as *managerialism*?

The answer we would give is that collaboration may not be compatible with managerialism, but then we would also argue that managerialism is not the same thing as effective management! What we mean by this is that the term managerialism is usually taken to denote an obsessive preoccupation with systems of control. This kind of mechanistic, inward-looking approach to management is quite out of tune with current thinking about what makes for an effective management system.

The new orthodoxy emphasizes that the most effective organizations are likely to be ones in which small, highly autonomous units are in constant communication with the outside world and in which managers manage not by diktat, but by developing a shared sense of values and commitments (Peters and Waterman, 1982, pp. 89–118). This is precisely the direction collaboration is likely to take any organization and leads us to believe that its principles and practices can be fully integrated into modern management cultures without any need to compromise on basic principles.

Beyond the public and the private

One feature shared by both collectivism and contract culture is the acceptance of a fundamental distinction between the private and the public domains of community care. Both collectivism and contract culture assume that there is a basic divide between the private world of what has come to be called 'informal care' and the domain of the state or the market. These domains are seen to operate according to very different principles and the result is community care policies which effectively fail to address the everyday reality in which the private and public domains intermingle and 'interweave' (Bayley, 1978, p. 31).

On the other hand, one strength of the collaborative approach is that it is applicable across the whole range of community care situations, especially those which straddle the private/public domain. In fact, collaborative principles form the essential bedrock of those interwoven social support networks which are so characteristic of community care and which consist of service users, their friends, relatives and neighbours, domiciliary care services, health and social work practitioners and others.

Collaboration in practice

It is now time to apply some of this thinking to community care practice. A hypothetical example will help us to do this.

A social worker and a district nurse have been working in the same locality for five years. Their offices are situated about a mile from one another and they spend much of their time visiting and working with the same section of the local population: older people and those relatives, friends and neighbours involved in supporting them.

Let us suppose that, in all that time, the social worker and the district nurse have had no face-to-face contact. This continues to be the case even though they are currently working with the same person, Ms Anderson, a woman of 85 who is partially sighted, with severe arthritis, supported mainly by her daughter but also visited occasionally by her son.

Although it was the district nurse who initiated the referral about Ms Anderson which led to the involvement of the social worker, she did so in writing and did not follow it up with any direct contact. In the past, the social worker has made referrals to the district nurse in exactly the same kind of impersonal fashion.

Both the social worker and the nurse see their roles with service users and carers as that of 'experts'. Neither of them attaches much value to the views of those they work with. If they had been asked, they would have justified this by arguing that while they have an obligation to obtain as much information as possible about 'problems', they alone have the knowledge and skill to solve these problems because they are qualified professionals.

For her part, Ms Anderson is not very happy with either the general approach or the attitudes of these two practitioners. She feels she was not consulted about the referral to the social worker, which focused on her 'need' for a day centre. If asked she would have said that she did not want to go to a day centre but would like to have discussed ways in which she could go shopping and visit friends more frequently. Instead she was forced to explain this to the social worker when she first visited, but got the impression that the social worker was not really listening to her because the conversation kept returning to the subject of day centres.

Most of us would have little difficulty in recognizing that this is not an example of collaboration. The practitioners are isolated from one another and do things *to* elderly people and their families and friends, rather than *with* them. Ms Anderson experiences her relationship with them as quite oppressive. She has not complained about her treatment, but only because she has not been made aware that she has the right to complain and she would be worried about doing so. The non-collaborative stance of the social worker and the district nurse is supported by a very traditional kind of professional belief system which lays claim to a specific and exclusive body of knowledge and skill. It follows from this that neither of them recognizes any accountability other than to their own organizations and line managers.

While the pattern of care in this situation fails almost every test of quality and value for money imaginable, managing to be both ineffective and oppressive at the same time, it also has a self-perpetuating quality which means that change is unlikely to be generated from within the system. We list some of the features associated with it below. Although they are drawn directly from this particular example, we would suggest that they are in fact characteristic of a certain kind of community care system.

The isolated expert system

The isolated expert system is associated with:

- High levels of professional power.
- A traditional professional belief system based on the notion of the professional as expert.
- Indirect communication between practitioners.
- Poor communication with, and little notice taken of, service users.
- Little or no communication between practitioners and carers or others involved in the situation.
- Resistance to change.
- Line management accountability only (no accountability to service users and carers).

But what if the social worker and district nurse find that they are constantly getting in each other's way? What if one arrives to visit at the same time as the other, or they both quite separately decide to contact two local volunteer organizations to ask for a volunteer to visit and two different volunteers turn up? What if Ms Anderson, perhaps encouraged by her son on one of his visits, finally begins to challenge the quality of the service she is getting and the way she is being treated? What if her daughter, as the key carer involved, also complains about these things – the fact that nobody has spoken to her about her needs and that there is so much confusion between the practitioners that her mother is becoming quite distressed?

The chances are that there might then have to be a change. It is likely that the practitioners might start having more contact with one another and with Ms Anderson's son and daughter. But it is also likely that this pattern of contact would be of a reactive nature, oriented towards resolving one particular problem after another and characterized by a high level of acrimony and continuing problems of communication. There is no reason to believe that either the general approach or the attitudes of the practitioners to one another and to the family would change.

Again, most of us would have little difficulty in recognizing that this is not an example of collaboration. Although there is a lot more contact between all those involved than in the first scenario, there is little evidence of any change in underlying values or beliefs and no evidence of any attempt at cooperation. We would argue that all this is characteristic of a certain kind of community care system which we describe below.

The conflict-laden system

This system is associated with:

- High levels of professional power.
- A traditional professional belief system.
- Direct but reactive communication between practitioners.
- Confused and inadequate communication between practitioners and service users.
- Poor communication between practitioners and carers or others involved in the situation.
- Instability.
- Line management accountability only.

So far, we have explored two extreme forms of non-collaborative activity – one characterized by isolated expert activity, the other by conflict and confusion. However, it does not follow that simply avoiding one or the other of these extremes ensures a collaborative outcome.

Let us suppose that the social worker and the district nurse in the second example are encouraged by their managers to reduce the level of conflict and confusion to manageable proportions by redefining the boundaries of their respective roles in more appropriate ways, such as meeting with one another if there are problems and providing more information to service users and carers to enable them to challenge decisions they are unhappy about in a more planned and formal way. This package of measures might well succeed in improving the situation. But although isolation on the one hand and conflict and confusion on the other have been avoided, has collaboration actually been generated?

The answer must surely be no. There is still no sense of any attempt to establish what we have referred to as collaboration culture. Ms Anderson may now be more able to complain but she is no more able to influence assessment and care planning than before. No initiative has yet been taken to assess the needs of her daughter and it is not clear how she might contribute to the process of planning future support for her mother. Likewise the social worker and district nurse may have created new mechanisms for solving problems, but they have not created any opportunities for sharing their perceptions; there has been no attempt to work out common goals or shared processes of planning and organizing work; and there is nothing in place which would enable tasks to be shared.

Although there is more emphasis on accountability, it is defined strictly in terms of service provision. There is no evidence of any attempt to create a sense of shared accountability for the way in which the work is undertaken. Finally, although the 'expert' belief system has been played down in the search for ways of reducing conflict, it has not been effectively challenged and still underpins day-to-day activity, effectively disempowering service users and carers.

Arguably, the biggest obstacle to the development of collaborative work lies not in the first two scenarios, but in the final one. Here the extremes of isolation, conflict and confusion have been avoided or overcome, but there is little or no evidence of what we have called collaboration culture and the pressure for change has been reduced.

It is all too easy to interpret relative peace and quiet as collaboration – particularly now when the terms 'collaboration' and 'partnership' are on everyone's lips – and therefore for all of us to convince ourselves, and attempt to convince others, that we are collaborating when we are simply co-existing. All these characteristics are representative of a third type of non-collaborative community care system.

Managed care

The managed care system is associated with:

- High levels of professional power.
- A traditional professional belief system.
- Direct, systematic but reactive communication between practitioners.
- Clear but limited and reactive communication between service users and practitioners.
- Clear but limited and reactive communication between practitioners and carers or others involved in the situation.
- Complacency.
- Some limited accountability to others apart from line managers.

In contrast, bearing in mind our provisional definition of collaboration and the issues raised by the example we have just given, it seems reasonable to believe that any set of community care arrangements claiming to be collaborative would have to satisfy certain criteria. Putting these together enables us to begin to glimpse what a collaborative community care system might look like.

Collaborative support

This kind of system is associated with:

- Acknowledgement of issues of power and control and attempts to empower service users, carers and others in less powerful positions.
- A collaborative belief system.
- Direct, pro-active communication between practitioners.
- Direct pro-active communication with service users.
- Direct pro-active communication with carers or others involved.
- Change and responsiveness.
- Multiple accountability (accountability to all those involved including service users and carers).

Summary

In this chapter we have looked at the relationship between collaboration and other aspects of community care. We have explored some of the conflicts and misunderstandings associated with ideas such as empowerment, partnership and collaboration and then pointed to the need for a new approach which recognizes the links between the involvement of users and carers and the development of effective patterns of inter-agency and inter-professional working. Collaboration is much more than a particular activity which might be undertaken from time to time for particular reasons. It has been argued that there is such a thing as collaboration culture which is very different to contract culture, but which has a similar potential to transform community care policy and practice at every level.

2 New skills for a new culture

Responding to the challenge

If there is to be a cultural revolution associated with collaboration in community care, we can now see that it must focus on power sharing and relationship building, and it must take place in a complex practice environment in which there is much that is pulling in very different directions. How is this going to be achieved? One answer is through training. But what is needed is not a quick technical fix, rather something which recognizes the fundamental nature of the issues involved.

This was the challenge which we sought to address through a project called Developing Collaborative Skills for Community Care. In the following sections we describe how the project came about and how we sought to put our initial ideas into practice.

Background to the project

We approached several local social work agencies, one of which in turn approached a local health authority, and in this way the Collaborative Skills in Community Care Project Consortium emerged.

We received a small grant from the Central Council for Education and Training in Social Work and set to work.

Culture or competency?

Early on in the life of the project, we recognized that there was a tension between what we saw as the essentially cultural nature of the challenges posed by community care and the dominant traditions of skills analysis.

We saw skill as grounded in a whole set of assumptions about the nature of professional role and identity. But the contemporary emphasis on an ability to evidence 'competence' through a specific, pre-determined set of outcomes (Central Council for Education and Training in Social Work, 1989) seemed to ignore the need to contextualize questions of skill.

Our concern with the relationship between skill and culture led us to formulate a different kind of approach, which retained a commitment to the idea of 'knowing in practice' (Schon, 1983, p. viii), which is associated with the competency-based approach, but which paid attention to a number of key issues all linked in one way or another with the idea that collaborative skills were likely to form part of a coherent practice culture.

We wanted to produce something which was not imposed on practice but grew out of it. In so doing, we wished to ensure that the experiences of those directly involved in community care were clearly represented in the contemporary debate; we were astonished at the relative lack of interest which had been displayed in what people were actually doing, what they thought about it and what they wanted in the future.

We did not want to produce an account of key skills which was so lengthy and complex that nobody would ever be able to make effective use of it to develop their own practice. In the context of community care, this was a real risk. There are so many different kinds of collaborative activity that any concept of 'core skills' will tend to disappear. This is similar to the problem some have encountered when trying to define care management tasks and skills – the problem of the 'Swiss army penknife' where the practitioner is meant to be 'not only a good assessor of individual need, but also a local community worker, service developer, budget manager, computer programmer, advocate, and possibly staff manager, as well' (Peck, Ritchie and Smith, 1992, p. 35). We sought to overcome this syndrome by focusing on the collaborative process itself.

There are many different views about community care even among those most intimately concerned with it. We did not want to assume a false consensus at the beginning but rather work towards building one towards the end of the project. We felt that no one group could lay claim to speaking for others and that it followed from this that we needed to involve users, carers, social workers and nurses in the project. We would have liked to involve other groups as well but had to recognize that this would be impractical.

Finally, we felt it might not be easy for those practitioners who were directly involved in community care to describe what they do and why they do it, or for service users and carers to say how they experienced the things that practitioners do and what they value most about them. Culture is often implicit rather than explicit. But, in our view, the opportunity of working together with others was likely to provide a context in which these implicit assumptions and values could be made explicit.

Putting all these points together we drew the obvious conclusion about collaborative skills, which was that they can only be analysed in a collaborative way.

Aims

Having clarified these basic points we felt able to draw up a statement of our aims. These were to:

> **Identify a culture and a core of skills associated with a collaborative approach to community care and rooted in the day-to-day experiences of service users, carers and community care practitioners, which were meaningful to and valued by all of them.**

We used the term 'practitioners' to denote both those involved in direct face-to-face work with service users and carers and those involved in facilitating this work as managers. As far as we were concerned, both groups were practitioners in the sense that they were both involved in the community care practice system, whether directly or indirectly. To talk about practice without reference to management, or to management without reference to practice, seemed to us to be nonsensical, especially in relation to community care.

As we were engaged in a small-scale project, there was a strict limit to the number of people with whom we could work. The particular practitioners we chose to work with were nurses and social workers. But from the beginning, we recognized that many of the issues identified by the project would be likely to be ones relevant to other professional groups, as well as to those such as home helps who might not constitute a traditional profession but who play a vital role in community care.

Networking and involvement

In looking to translate our aims into action we were very influenced by two ideas: *networking* and *involvement*. To some extent, this was for very personal reasons. We were already very interested in these ideas. One of us had been engaged in promoting 'involvement' both as a researcher and a campaigner for many years. The other had been similarly engaged in promoting and writing about networking for a considerable time.

From the beginning, therefore, we had to acknowledge that we were not disinterested observers or commentators. These concepts meant something to us. We were committed to them as ways forward for community care, and we saw the development project as a way of helping others to be committed to them as well.

In the following sections we briefly outline the ways in which ideas about networking and involvement have contributed to our understanding of collaborative work and collaboration culture.

Networking

A new way of working together

During the late 1980s and early 1990s a new practice began to emerge, one drawing on the concept of informal and innovative relationships. Often, but not always, they were of an *ad hoc* nature, involving individuals, groups and organizations joined to one another in ways which encouraged communication, cooperation and new opportunities for choice and empowerment. Increasingly, people began to refer to this approach as 'networking'.

The focus was on:

- Enabling interpersonal relationships to grow in contexts where trust was often a scarce commodity.
- Actively promoting a sense of involvement in collective endeavour and thereby enabling those involved to meet one another's needs or at least share one another's problems.
- Replacing fixed expectations with a commitment to flexibility and informality.
- Enhancing the growth of communication networks.
- Mobilizing people and resources (Trevillion, 1992, pp. 36–37).

Originally associated with community social work and community development, networking has come to be seen as a central issue in community care.

Networking and care management

Care management is often associated exclusively with 'purchasing' and by extension 'contract culture'. But it is also concerned with identifying need and 'co-ordinating' services (Austin, 1983, p. 16), and as such has generated a renewed interest in processes of inter-agency collaboration and collaboration with service users and carers. For example, it has been suggested that:

> an empowering approach to assessment and care management has to recognise that assessment involves an understanding of a social situation, of the pattern of relationships in which a person's needs are perceived by somebody as not being met. It is not just the assessment of an individual but of the relationship between them and the people with the resources to support or to change the situation (Smale and others, 1993, p. 43).

More generally, it has been argued that care management is concerned with 'building up linkages' (Payne, 1993, p. 2):

> Among the main elements of case management are: developing a range of alternative services which can be called into play for particular people; using the network of services and contacts in a community to identify people in need; negotiating and bringing together services in a package that works; following up the way in which services work together; and adapting this work as services, needs, and preferences change and checking and evaluating how the services work together. All this obviously makes developing the skills of working together with informal carers and other services a more central part of social work than it is with many conventional casework services (Payne, 1993, p. 3).

It is these and other aspects of care management which have brought networking to the fore in discussions about community care.

From the multi-disciplinary team to the collaborative network

Among professionals, particularly those working in health settings there has recently been an upsurge of interest in inter-professional collaboration, not just because of community care but because of the renewed interest in community-based 'primary health care'. Primary health care has been described as 'nurses, doctors, social workers and therapists working together to provide co-ordinated services' (Jones, 1992, p. 25).

But this interest has been accompanied by an increasing realization that the concept of the 'primary care team' may be quite misleading. The classic image of a team is of a tightly knit group of professionals with a fixed membership and a clearly defined set of common tasks. But it has become increasingly obvious that team boundaries in the real world are not fixed in this way.

There is no longer any agreement on what constitutes a primary health care team. In fact, it has been argued that different tasks will often require different teams (Jones, 1992, p. 26), and it is becoming clear that what health professionals appear to associate with teamwork is not a fixed structure or a fixed task but more dynamic and less tangible concepts such as patterns of 'roles, relationships, communication and mutual understanding' (Hutchinson and Gordon, 1992, p. 37).

It is these kind of considerations which are leading to a shift of focus away from the notion of multi-disciplinary teamwork towards the notion of developing collaborative multi-disciplinary networks. Because it is more flexible, the concept of the collaborative network can be extended much further than the older concept of teamwork. It is perhaps no exaggeration to say that this shift marks a sea change in attitudes to working together for community care. With the shift to the concept of the collaborative network comes a commitment to a new vision of community care as a set of open-ended and participative relationships linking practitioners, carers and service users together in a mutually beneficial and more or less integrated way.

Networking and the project

In general, we saw networking as important because its emergence signalled a willingness to rethink all kinds of taken-for-granted professional ideas in the search for effective forms of collaboration, and because it seemed to be based on a set of ideas which effectively opened up community care systems of all kinds to processes of involvement, communication and power sharing.

Involvement and empowerment

The second strand, or discourse, informing this project, that of involvement and empowerment, is a much broader one than that of community care professionals' growing interest in networking.

Since the 1970s people who use community care services have increasingly set up their own groups and organizations, such as organizations of disabled people, people with learning difficulties, older people, people with mental distress and people affected by HIV. There are now a large and growing number of such organizations. They operate at local, regional, national and international levels.

These groups are increasingly seeing themselves as part of a movement, identifying themselves with other new social movements, including the gay and lesbian, women's and black people's movements, and pointing to their shared characteristics and goals. They share a number of key qualities with such new social movements. For instance, they:

- Experience institutionalized social oppression.
- Recognize and value their own particular history and culture, and frame their activities in political terms.
- 'Come out' about themselves and assert their identity instead of trying to keep 'in the closet'.
- Take a pride in who they are.

Oliver offers a helpful description of the new social movements:

These movements have been seen as constituting the social basis for new forms of transformative political change. These social movements are 'new' in the sense that they are not grounded in traditional forms of political participation through the party system or single issue pressure group activity targetted at political decision-makers.

Instead they are culturally innovative in that they are part of the underlying struggle for genuine participatory democracy, social equality and justice, which has arisen out of 'the crisis in industrial culture'. These new social movements are consciously engaged in critical evaluation of capitalist society and in the creation of alternative models of social organisation at local, national and international levels, as well as trying to reconstruct the world ideologically and to create alternative forms of service provision (Oliver, 1990, p. 13).

He also identifies four characteristics associated with them. These are:

- They tend to be located at the periphery of the traditional political system and sometimes are deliberately marginalized.
- They offer a critical evaluation of society as part of 'a conflict between a declining but still vigorous form of domination and newly emergent forms of opposition'.
- They are concerned with the quality of people's lives as well as materialist needs.
- They tend to focus on issues that cross national boundaries and thus they become internationalist (Oliver, 1990, p. 118 and following).

Participation and empowerment are central philosophies underpinning the new social movements. They are an explicit expression of their concern with a different politics: a participatory politics. This is particularly developed in the disability and community care service users' movements. Shakespeare suggests that it may be more helpful to see the disabled people's movement as a *liberation* movement rather than a new social movement, emphasizing that:

> Liberation must involve the most widespread possible action and mobilisation, rather than mere changes in elites or legislation (Shakespeare, 1993, p. 53).

People are concerned with speaking and acting *for themselves*. It is a primary concern. It extends beyond the involvement of their constituency to the active involvement of as many members of it as possible. Service users' organizations are concerned with securing people's rights as citizens and service users.

While service users and their organizations have played a central part in the development of the discourse about participation in community care in Britain, it would be wrong to suggest that they have been the only voice arguing for involvement. There have been other pressures for change, most notably from successive Conservative governments committed to an expanded role for the market in the provision of welfare and a changed welfare economy (Croft and Beresford, 1992, pp. 30–31).

The consumerist and democratic approaches

The diversity of interest in involvement has meant that there has not been any consensus in the conception or definition of 'involvement'. Instead two main approaches to user involvement are increasingly identified: the 'consumerist' and the 'democratic' approaches. While there are some overlaps between the two, they reflect different philosophies and objectives. The first has been associated with the politics of the new right and the second with the emergence of rights', self-advocacy, disabled people's and users' organizations. Both these approaches may have their merits, but they should not be confused. They are very different.

The emergence of consumerist thinking on health and welfare services has coincided with the expansion of commercial provision and political pressure for a changed economy of welfare. The discussion of participation has been overlaid with the language of consumerism and the concerns of the market. Consumerism starts with the idea of buying the goods and services we want instead of making collective provision for them.

In the debate about user involvement, while the consumerist approach has tended to come from service providers and to address their concerns and the needs of services, for example improving management to achieve greater economy, efficiency and effectiveness, the democratic approach has largely been developed by service users and their organizations. As we have said, what distinguishes these organizations from traditional pressure groups is that they seek to *speak for themselves* instead of other groups speaking on their behalf.

Here the primary concern has been with empowerment, the redistribution of power and people gaining more say and control over their lives.

The democratic approach is not service-centred. It is about much more than having a voice in services, however important that may be. It is concerned with how we are treated and regarded more generally; with the achievement of people's civil rights and equality of opportunity. This is reflected in the three current priorities of the disabled people's movement: for anti-discriminatory legislation, a freedom of information act and the funding and resourcing of organizations controlled by disabled people themselves.

Service users and collaborative networking

Collaborative networking has not yet figured as a major concept in the theoretical and philosophical discussions of service users' and carers' organizations. Concepts of involvement, empowerment, advocacy, rights, discrimination and oppression have been much more central to debates and developments. Yet networking is actually a central concern and activity of such groups and organizations, in terms of both their support and campaigning activities. A lot of networking goes on among service users and their organizations. There is recognition among such groups of the importance of networking and many efforts are being made to develop new and effective approaches to it. At the same time lack of resources is placing major obstacles in the way of:

- Networking within disability movements.
- Networking between disability movements.
- Regional and national networking.
- International networking.
- Networking between service users and carers (Beresford, 1993).

Any exploration of collaborative and networking skills in community care needs to take account both of the networking needs of service users and carers and the importance of challenging constraints in the way of meeting them.

Putting the project together

Although debates about networking have developed separately from debates about involving service users and carers, we felt that it was time to begin to develop a more integrated profile of the skills needed for all forms of collaborative work. We even came up with a provisional definition of collaborative skills which would give substance to this belief and provide us with a focus:

> **The skills which are characteristically deployed when developing and sustaining those networks of communication, cooperation and empowerment integral to 'good practice' in community care.**

And yet, we felt there were good reasons to hold back from a fully integrated approach to the analysis of collaborative skills.

The whole purpose of the project was to find out more about both collaboration culture and collaboration skills. By acting as if we already knew the answers when we only knew the questions, it seemed likely that we would fatally undermine what we were trying to do. This was not a purely technical, methodological point. There were issues of power and control involved. We wanted to involve service users and carers as well as practitioners. But any attempt to define one specific set of skills or even topics for discussion would almost certainly have led the project to be disproportionately influenced by professional concerns.

A context of contested concepts

This is particularly important bearing in mind the diversity of views about community care that exists. We wanted to take account of this in the project. The new thinking about community care has not resulted in any consensus about it. Instead very real differences are emerging in language, ideology and understanding. These differences mainly reflect the different ideas and discussions of service users and providers – service professionals and disabled people.

We feel it is important both to identify these differences and for this discussion to take account of them. This book is concerned with collaboration, but that does not mean denying difference where it exists. Instead the aim should be to try and be clearer about it and recognize its implications. In our view it is only the kind of collaborative approach which we have tried to explore which makes it possible to reconcile the perspectives of service users, carers and service workers. It is this which has led us to such an approach.

Care management: an extension of the old paternalism or a new approach to practice?

Some service users have called the care management approach to community care into question. The community care reforms in Britain have entailed a changed model of statutory practice. Traditionally the 'practitioner' was expected to work out what help the 'client' wanted and provide it, generally from a narrow menu of services provided by their agency, like home help, day services and residential accommodation.

The new model of practice is meant to start from and be much more explicitly led by the needs of the service user. It is framed in terms of the idea of 'care management'. The care manager may now be drawn from a wide range of practitioners, including nurses, social workers, occupational therapists and home care organizers. There are three key components to care management: assessment, creating a 'care package' of support, and review.

This approach has two rationales. First, the aim is to generate more responsive, flexible and imaginative forms of support and move away from the service-led model that has characterized community care and personal social services more generally. Service-led policy and practice meant that service users have often had to fit into services, instead of services matching service users. Second, much more emphasis is to be given to making the most cost-effective use of budgets in order to provide support as efficiently and economically as possible. Budgetary considerations and responsibilities are built into care management, where before they were not seen as part of the duty or role of the community care practitioner.

A problem has quickly emerged with these two objectives. Instead of being complementary, they frequently seem to be at odds with each other. Service agencies and service users' organizations both argue that services frequently seem to be budget-driven rather than needs-led. But the problem of finance taking priority over need is not the only concern raised by service users and their organizations.

They have developed a more fundamental critique of the care management approach to practice. Many are dissatisfied with the terminology and the business model underpinning it. Disabled people's and other service user organizations increasingly reject the notion of 'care'. Care is associated with custody, being controlled and their own lack of control. Many disabled people feel the word has a history which is demeaning and based on an assumption of their dependence. They talk about the way 'care' services medicalize them and treat them as sick or as a problem (Beresford and Croft, 1993a, p. 35).

The use of the term *care management* is another expression of the current fashion for the new business culture in welfare. It may be intended to mean ensuring people get the support they need and overseeing the services they receive. But for many service users it carries different resonances. They dislike the idea of being managed, as if they cannot manage their own lives or as if they were an object to be managed.

It is not only the terminology which service users are questioning. They are also challenging the framework underlying it. They are developing a different framework for meeting their needs which puts them in the driving seat and means that effectively they become their own care manager. This can be seen in each aspect of the care management process.

Therefore, in assessment, instead of an outside professional deciding what a service user's needs are – which is how it has traditionally been and how it is still often the case as care management is conventionally interpreted – the service user defines their own needs for themselves. Such self-assessment makes possible self-defined needs. The role of the worker here is to support people with information, advocacy and support.

Instead of the care manager putting together a 'care package' for the service user, service users can set up their own self-run support schemes. Already a number of disabled people run their own personal assistance schemes. They put these together themselves or with assistance. They control them, the schemes are accountable to them and they hire and fire workers.

Finally, the service user has the key say in review. Review is explicitly based on their judgement, their criteria and their experience, rather than those of the worker involved.

Clearly such a user-led model of community care has major implications for the role of both the care manager and other community care workers. It means a continuing role, but a different role to that suggested by the terminology, which puts the professional centre stage. Some professional reservations have been raised about this user-led model of care management. Commentators have suggested that some service users would be unable to undertake their own assessment of needs, because of intellectual or other impairment, for example, people suffering from Alzheimer's disease.

Disabled people argue that with suitable support *all* service users can be involved in communicating what they want. Care management can thus be seen as a continuum, from some service users taking the main responsibility for arranging the meeting of their needs, to others being involved as fully as they wish in the process by a practitioner acting on their behalf. So instead of care manager as mediator or arbiter between the service user's needs and the support provided, the care manager becomes a supporter to enable the service user to work out what support they want and how best it could be provided to meet their needs.

Carers

The concept of 'carer' is also a contested one. It emerged in the 1970s to reflect the work of millions of people, predominantly women, who support disabled, ill, old and distressed people unpaid at home, often without choice or adequate support and with restrictions on their opportunities and rights. Since then there has been an increasing emphasis in government policy on the role of unpaid carers. Some critics argue that this has extended to substituting their work for public provision.

In the project on which this book draws, we spoke to both service users and carers and sought to identify and distinguish their views and concerns while recognizing that service users may also be carers and carers service users.

As there has been increasing recognition of the role of carers, service users have identified problems with it. A common complaint is that more weight is paid to the views of carers than of service users 'because it's the cheaper option', and that the service system has frequently encouraged carers to speak for service users and failed to distinguish between the two. Disabled people increasingly demand choice in the support they receive instead of having to rely on partners, family or friends as carers. Disabled people are now beginning to question the basic idea of the carer. For example:

> Informal carers only exist as an oppressed social group because older and disabled people experience social, economic and political oppression ... These are the factors which create a dependence on unpaid assistance within the family (Morris, 1993).

This clearly has important implications for both community care policy and practice, since it suggests that if the prior needs of disabled people and other service users are met, then the support they receive on the basis of personal relationships and the needs of those offering such support are likely to change. It is also a further reminder of the need for services and practitioners to respect the rights and choices of both service users and of people who offer them support, as well as recognizing the differences between them.

The plan

The different views of service users, carers and workers about community care, as well as the differences in power between them, led us to conceive of the development project in a particular way.

We chose a model which could be described as that of two streams flowing into one another at the final stage. One stream was to consist of work with service users and carers; the other stream was to consist of work with social workers and nurses. The whole process was to culminate in a workshop in which all groups would participate.

This plan was heavily influenced by our concern with ensuring that the process of exploring collaboration culture and collaborative skills was itself a collaborative process.

Keeping work with service users and carers separate initially from work with social workers and nurses was seen as a way of opening up rather than closing down the communication process. It was hoped that it would create opportunities for people to develop their own ideas in their own ways prior to meeting with one another to discuss them. But we recognized that this made the planned workshop session all the more important.

Although it was to consist of a one-off event, the workshop was seen as very significant to the whole project. In particular we anticipated that it would produce three gains:

1   Opportunities for the different groups of participants in the project to learn more about one another's perspectives.
2   The chance for participants themselves to be able to negotiate and synthesize their different perspectives.
3   The possibility of developing a skills profile for community care collectively 'owned' by them all.

Overall, we saw the project as a development project in that we hoped that all those taking part would be able to raise their levels of awareness about collaboration; that service users and carers would become clearer about what it was that they had a right to expect from practitioners; and practitioners might have an opportunity to think more deeply than they otherwise would about the knowledge, values and skills that they brought to their collaborative work and how these might be most effectively developed.

Summary

This chapter has looked at the background, aims and early stages of the Collaborative Skills in Community Care Project and in so doing has explored a number of key concepts, such as the relationship between competency, skills and culture. We have also tried to acknowledge the intellectual antecedents of the project and in particular to show how both that broad current of thinking about relationship building, often referred to as networking, and ideas about the involvement of service users and carers, influenced it. Finally, there has been an attempt in this chapter to show how the project was put together and why it assumed the shape it did.

3 The community care diaries: a record of collaboration

An inter-professional project?

Although we decided to separate the first phase of our work with service users and carers from our work with practitioners, we did not separate the social workers, community psychiatric nurses, district nurses or managers taking part in the project from one another. In fact, as far as we were concerned, collaboration and a certain kind of inter-professionalism were inextricably entwined and we intended the project to reflect this.

We have not been the only ones to recognize a link between inter-professional work and collaboration. For example:

> Since 1985 a number of key organisations have been established whose main aim is to foster collaboration and communication between professionals. ... The aims, objectives and mission statements of all of these organisations bring out as watchwords the three C's: communication, collaboration, and – much more difficult to achieve – co-operation (Spratley and Pietroni, 1994, p. 2).

This link is not confined to collaboration between professionals. The emphasis on communication, collaboration and cooperation so evident in inter-professional work has led to a phenomenon described by Spratley and Pietroni as the 'user centredness' of inter-professional work (Spratley and Pietroni, 1994, p. 17).

And yet, when groups of different professionals come together to discuss skills, they still tend to treat issues such as multi-disciplinary teamwork as if they benefit service users but have little to do with processes by which service users and carers might themselves become part of the team.

We wanted our work with practitioners to be somewhat different. We did not want to encourage them to focus exclusively on their relationships with

COLEG MENAI
BANGOR, GWYNEDD LL57 2TP

one another or other professionals, but to keep in mind the connections between all forms of collaboration. In this way, we hoped to open up the whole question of skills analysis to a broader set of concerns and issues. At the same time we felt we would not be imposing an artificial constraint on their discussions. On the contrary, it seemed to us that so many inter-professional issues also involved relationships with service users and carers that it would be artificial to attempt to separate them.

Methods

Our approach was shaped by our overall aims and by some specific con-cerns. Because we saw our work as akin to stimulating a discussion, we were interested less in collecting data from nurses and social workers than in raising awareness of collaboration and the skills involved in it. But as our central concerns were with 'knowing in practice' (Schon, 1983, p. viii), we did want to ensure that any discussions were grounded in practice realities rather than idealized images. We decided that the best way of proceeding was to focus on day-to-day collaborative practice through a *community care diary* and then to develop ideas about these practices through *discussion groups*.

All participants were asked to keep a community care diary for one month. This chapter is largely concerned with the subject matter contained in the diaries. In the following chapter, however, the focus shifts to the discussion groups which were intended to provide opportunities for par-ticipants to learn from one another, make new links and critically evaluate existing practices.

The practitioners

Sixteen participants were recruited for the research project. They consisted of social workers employed by one London borough, and nurses employed by a district health authority covering the same area. Some were employed in direct work with service users/patients. Others were employed in man-agement roles. For some, their main area of interest was in the field of mental distress. For others, the professional focus was ageing. Two de-scribed themselves as African–Caribbean, one described himself as Asian. Three out of the original 16 were male. One of the white female participants had a visual impairment.

Although we did not contact particular individuals, we quite deliberately sought to make contact with professionals who already had a strong interest in collaborative work and in community care. The demands we then made on their time ensured that only those with high levels of commitment actually saw the whole research process through from start to finish.

The introductory workshop

All those who expressed an interest in participating in the project were invited to an introductory workshop. This was designed to encourage people to ask questions and to enable them to raise specific concerns prior to making any commitment to the project. It also allowed us to begin engaging at a personal level and in a collaborative way with those with whom we would be working closely later on.

Drop-out rate

One of the original male participants withdrew immediately after the workshop and several others did not fill in their diaries because of work pressures. In all, six diaries were completed and two group interviews and one individual interview were held.

Perhaps rather perversely, we were pleased that some individuals felt able to withdraw from the project immediately after the workshop having realized what it would entail. Those who stayed with the project to the end demonstrated considerable commitment. However, it was disappointing that the six professionals who completed their diaries and attended discussion groups were all white.

Reading the community care diaries

As the completed diaries were returned to us, we began to read them and identify issues which needed to be followed up in discussion. As we did so, we became increasingly aware that hidden beneath the surface detail of particular meetings or telephone conversations was a critical mass of ideas, attitudes and values strongly influencing behaviour. In what follows we attempt to identify some of the key elements of this critical mass.

To protect confidentiality, the examples which are given correspond to but are not identical with the situations described by the professionals.

Concepts of need

Any attempt to develop a profile of skills related to community care has to start with the key concept of 'need'. Perceptions of need are not only important in themselves but also because of their impact on assessment, planning and all subsequent judgements about effectiveness. This applies as much to perceptions about the need for service development or better inter-agency communication or community needs as it does to perceptions of individual needs. The diaries tended to focus on the latter, but other kinds of needs were also mentioned and in every case the kind of assumptions made about them influenced the whole process of assessment and intervention.

The service-led model

For both social workers and nurses, descriptions of need sometimes took the form of a list of problems relating to specific services in a straightforward one-to-one fashion, such as 'help with cooking and cleaning', or even of formal care or medical services which might be appropriate, such as 'day care' or 'wound treatment'. In these cases, there was often no clear separation between the general concept of need and the more focused concept of 'service requirement'. As the community care reforms have been largely based on precisely this kind of separation between needs assessment and service provision, this seemed to suggest that rather more traditional concepts of assessment were still influential in at least some situations.

The diaries suggested that where there was such a blurring of the distinction between need and service requirement, there was also a very clearly defined problem which helped to shape perceptions of the situation and expectations of the role of the professional, as when, for instance, helping someone to move from an institution into the community. It was almost as if in such situations the social worker or nurse was presented with a ready-made task which they had to perform in a relatively short space of time and this precluded any attempt at comprehensive needs assessment.

While the service-oriented type of assessment was the most limited in terms of scope for professional judgement, it was also, rather paradoxically, the least democratic type of assessment. It seemed to be least informed by any concept of assessment as a process of consulting about issues and options with service users and carers. The impression given was of a process characterized instead by a narrow focus on key tasks or one problem, such as poor housing, which the professional was expected to solve.

Further evidence that the issue of expectations of role was connected with the way in which the concept of need was understood was contained in the way in which statutory responsibilities were identified with the concept of need, so that, for example, a responsibility to devise a 'Section 117 after-care plan' was offered as a definition of need.

The service-oriented type of assessment was characterized by a very limited concept of the needs of the support network. Where relatives or friends were mentioned it was often in terms of things they would not do for the service user, such as 'daughter and son-in-law do not wish to have father home', rather than in ways which suggested their own needs were being explored.

Broadly speaking, these kind of assessments were dominated by a rather narrowly focused, problem-solving ethos.

The collaborative model

What was noticeable from the diaries was that while a minority of the assessments were dominated by a traditional service-led model, most were characterized by much more holistic approaches to the definition of need. Rather than simply imposing service perspectives these approaches were characterized by a much greater sensitivity to the different ways in which needs were experienced and expressed. At its simplest, this involved a recognition that more than one person in a situation could have needs. In one example of this kind, the needs identified included not just those of a disabled service user who needed help with 'daily activities', but those of his wife who needed to be able to share some of the practical tasks involved, thereby removing what was described as the responsibility of 'physical care' from her.

But this type of approach to assessment also took more complex forms in which there was evidence of a willingness to be very open-minded as to what might constitute need. In one situation need might be defined in terms of 'isolation, housing and financial problems'. In another situation, need was seen in terms of 'medical care and poor quality relationships'. This reflected a concern with persons rather than straightforward problem solving. This enabled skills, attitudes and levels of motivation to be seen from time to time as specific needs.

Sometimes, instead of listing specific needs in a quantitative way, the assessment focused on a key issue and the needs generated by it. One example of this way of thinking about need was enabling people to manage the transition from hospital to community. Here, need was perceived in terms of developing a support network. Interestingly, this linked the kind of needs someone might have in relation to quality of life with those they might have in coping with day-to-day problems in an integrated approach to the analysis of need. Where this approach was adopted it enabled the professionals to step back and think about the connections between all aspects of the situation.

As we read the diaries, it became clear to us that there was a link between holistic, needs-led perspectives and a predisposition to collaborative work. Not only were holistic assessments frequently a product of collaboration but the plans made as a result tended to emphasize the contributions that could be made by a wide range of different individuals and agencies.

Collaboration and innovation

It was noticeable that wherever the emphasis was on service innovation there was a tendency to adopt a needs-led/collaborative approach. While the traditional service-oriented assessment was exclusively concerned with the allocation of existing predetermined services, the collaborative approach was the norm when situations were assessed with a view to developing new kinds of services or new policies.

In one situation need was defined in terms of developing new shared policies to work with offenders who had been given a psychiatric diagnosis. In another situation need was defined in terms of developing shared understandings between different agencies in relation to care management and specific mention was made of the need for better cooperation and communication. This again emphasized the relationship between concepts of need and collaboration culture. A commitment to needs-led thinking seemed to lead naturally to an innovative and developmental orientation to service delivery and one which focused on collaborative initiatives of various kinds.

Identifying positives in the situation

Community care assessment involves thinking about the relationship between needs and resources in the context of a specific situation (Smale and others, 1993, p. 43). Therefore concepts about resources are every bit as important as concepts of need.

Resources as services

Frequently, practitioners identified particular services, such as housing or occupational therapy, as resources. At other times these services were represented by and identified with specific individuals, such as a community psychiatric nurse or a disabled employment adviser. Although sometimes the emphasis was more on unpaid assistance than formal services, the same notion of a resource as a fixed set of taken-for-granted services prevailed.

Within this broad definition of resource, there was some variation. For example, sometimes the service was anonymous, at other times it was individualized and personalized. As a result, agencies or professional groupings were sometimes identified as resources while at other times specific friends, family members or professional colleagues were named. Only in a small number of cases were attempts made to identify skills separately as resources. It is perhaps no accident that this occurred mainly in relation to areas of recognized expertise such as counselling rather than in the broad range of more practical supportive activities.

Resources as relationships and opportunities

The diaries showed that sometimes a very different approach was taken to the identification of resources. This more qualitative approach included as resources such things as a history of inter-agency cooperation and multi-disciplinary work, a supportive family and a tightly knit network of friends. It also included relatively intangible things such as 'opportunities' embedded in a situation, such as access to transport. Moreover, the process of mobilizing resources like this was described almost invariably in collaborative terms. The reasons for this were significant.

These resources were not things, they were not fixed or given. They could not be simply 'plugged in'. Rather they were outcomes of certain processes. Inter-agency cooperation would continue to be a resource only if agencies continued to relate well to one another. Families and friends would continue to be supportive only if they were able to get their needs met and if their relationships with one another and those they were supporting continued to be positive. Transport could be accessed only if geographical constraints and other kinds of restrictions were overcome. The process of mobilizing resources like this was inevitably very different from the process of simply asking for services. One of the distinguishing characteristics was that it always involved a process of negotiation leading to a process of collaboration. These were all collaborative resources or resources which emerged through a process of collaborative work.

Between two cultures: service-led versus collaborative approaches

Overall there were strong indications of a link between concepts of need, the way in which resources were described and the relative significance of collaborative approaches to community care practice.

The characteristic pattern was twofold. Where needs were seen in terms of service requirement there was a tendency to describe resources in somewhat mechanistic terms, either as part of the situation which could be taken for granted or as standard services of some kind which could be introduced into it.

But where, as in the majority of cases, needs were seen more holistically, then the concept of resource was extended more widely to include individuals and agencies with whom there would have to be negotiations about roles and relationships. In general in these situations, much less was taken for granted and a variety of different perspectives were assumed.

In general, assessment was characterized by two major approaches to the question of need and the question of resource: a traditional one associated with concepts of service requirement, and a needs-led, more holistic approach in which negotiation and collaboration formed part of the professional world-view.

It was not surprising to find two very different professional cultures present simultaneously, nor to find these combined in the same individuals. This kind of struggle between the old and the new is exactly what one would expect at a time of 'paradigm change' in professional attitudes and values (Kuhn, 1962). What was more surprising was that there seemed to be no particularly strong connection between professional background and approaches to assessment. Rather, it seemed to be the way in which the situation was perceived which triggered a particular stance towards these issues.

Perceptions of complexity

As we explored the comments people made in the diaries, it rapidly became clear that the relative dominance of the traditional service culture and the new needs-led collaborative culture in any particular situation was associated with the extent to which a situation was perceived to be 'complex'. This issue of complexity seemed to be a product of two separate but related considerations. Most straightforwardly, it represented a judgement about the need to manage a complex pattern of resources. But, on the other hand, it also represented a judgement about the non-standard or non-routine nature of the needs in question.

In general, where the focus was on a particular narrowly defined problem, assessment seemed to be oriented towards service requirements rather than broader concepts of need and there was little evidence of thinking about the relevance of collaboration except to some extent with the service user. Where situations were judged to be 'complex', on the other hand, then a collaborative approach came to the fore.

There were strong indications that running alongside the traditional, individualistic and problem-centred approach was another set of ideas which were not articulated very clearly but which seemed to recognize that situations were often complex and multi-faceted and could only be understood therefore by including all those involved. There was thus an implicit acknowledgement of the part others were likely to play both in terms of defining the situation and in terms of social support.

Understanding the process by which needs came to be understood as complex in this way was clearly the key to understanding how decisions came to be made about networking and collaboration in general. It was as if professionals asked themselves a number of questions before coming to a decision about complexity and whether or not they were going to spend time developing a collaborative network.

Were carers 'coping'?

In relation to individuals they saw as in need, one of the factors seemed to be the degree to which carers were seen to be able and willing to cope with only minor input from formal services. If they were judged to be coping then it was much less likely that the situation would be perceived as complex and as a result little or no consideration would be given to support and collaboration.

What was being said about caring and its relationship to perceptions of complexity and collaborative work seemed to us to be very important. It seemed to be informed by resource-led rather than needs-led thinking. While there were many situations in which formal services would be inappropriate or intrusive, the concept of coping seemed to function also as a way of rationing scarce resources. It did this in two ways.

First, and most straightforwardly, perceptions of degrees of coping among family and friends could be used to make decisions about services. Whether this way of rationing resources was official policy or not was unclear and may well have been irrelevant given the constraints imposed by a central government administration which took the view that family and friends represented the 'front line' of community care.

Second, the concept of whether carers were coping seemed to be not simply a way of rationing services; it was quite compatible with, for example, a decision to provide a specific service or set of services in accordance with what we have described as the traditional 'service requirement model'. Rather it seemed sometimes to be linked to a view that what made a situation complex and thus requiring of collaboration was the fact that the carers themselves needed support in order to cope.

To some extent this is self-evidently true. Supporting carers involves an objective increase in the complexity of the practice issues. But was it right to assume that someone who was coping did not need support? It seemed very much as if restricting the notion of 'need for support' to situations where coping was actually breaking down was leading to a reactive crisis-oriented model of community care practice. We were told later on that collaboration required investments of time and energy which were in very short supply and that these kinds of considerations were used to make decisions about priorities. There were therefore clear links between this and the next question.

Does this situation have a high priority?

It seemed likely that resource constraints played some part in deciding whether or not to take the time and trouble to develop a collaborative network in a particular situation. As well as the question of whether carers were coping, other factors, such as perceptions of risk and statutory responsibilities, would also inevitably play a part in the process of prioritizing work. At least some of the variation in what was and was not handled collaboratively could be accounted for in this way.

Were other professionals or other agencies involved?

Often it was the necessity to consult with other practitioners and other agencies and the need to access resources controlled by others which appeared strongly to influence the decision as to whether a situation was complex enough to be networked.

Do I have primary responsibility?

If individual professionals perceived that they had primary responsibility, then they were much more likely to take on the role of networker than if they saw someone else as having primary responsibility. This relationship between networking and primary responsibility seemed to be very significant because it implied that networking was strongly motivated by a concern with and a sense of accountability for outcomes.

Overall, what these questions reveal is that complexity was much less an objective feature of the situations these practitioners dealt with than an alternative approach to them triggered by a series of events which effectively made simple solutions impossible. In other words, as is often the case, these professionals found themselves working in new and creative ways when it was impossible to act in what one might describe as a routine manner.

This finding should come as no surprise. After all, we all of us tend to act routinely until something about the situation forces us to stop and think. In this context, the contrast between the two very different ways of working that was so characteristic of these practitioners becomes much more understandable.

Collaboration and power sharing

When we shifted our attention from the very general collaborative issues we have looked at so far to the specific issue of power sharing, the diaries became less informative.

On the one hand, most practitioners showed that they were willing to collaborate with a very wide range of people. In one fairly typical example, this included a service user, hostel staff and a consultant psychiatrist. On the other hand, there was little evidence of the extent to which professionals saw their own power as an issue for negotiation.

While many of the diary entries showed a well-developed awareness of inequality and injustice within society and a willingness to advocate on behalf of those who were oppressed, this awareness did not tend to be extended into an analysis of relationships between community care professionals and service users. There was little explicit reference to power and methods of power sharing with service users.

This did not necessarily mean that power sharing did not happen. It might simply have been unstated. Perhaps it was a 'basic assumption' and was so much a part of the assumptive world of the professionals that it literally went without saying. There was some evidence to support this idea, because the diaries showed that professionals seemed to accept that in general all those who were consulted had the right to influence decision making and many of the references to negotiation with service users, carers and other practitioners could be seen as coded references to power sharing. But, in general, power sharing was very much an implicit rather than explicit goal and was incorporated within an understandable concern with 'getting things done'.

It seemed to us that there might be real differences between this type of professional perspective on issues of power and control and the perspective of service users and carers. We decided to try to clarify some of these issues in the discussion groups.

Roles and modes of interaction

Fortunately the diaries were clearer in relation to a number of other issues, some of which cast a little more light on the subject of power sharing.

Coordination, mobilization and support emerged as central preoccupations of all the practitioners in relation to networking. When asked to reflect on their roles in relation to other members of the collaborative network, the words 'coordination', 'facilitation' and 'support' were frequently mentioned, often linked to one another, such as 'coordinating a support package'. At other times, more specific phrases were used, such as 'pulling together the network'. Sometimes these phrases were linked to particular goals, such as 'continuity of care' or more immediately 'attempting to improve relationships'.

It was not immediately apparent how much power or authority was vested in these roles. Sometimes the networker seemed to carry considerable if informal authority, as when devising and communicating 'daily plans', at other times the role seemed much more of a nurturing one, as when the role was described in terms of 'advice' or 'emotional support'.

The predominant tone was an active one although there were also references to acting as a 'resource' for members of the network.

For the most part these professionals were highly flexible, gearing their roles and modes of interaction to particular circumstances. There was thus considerable evidence of strategic thinking. There were some indications, however, that roles were not always freely chosen, often representing something of a compromise between what professionals would like to have done and what they felt able to do. For example, one professional commented that an inability to maintain contact at the planned level had led to a *de facto* change in her role and the setting of a much less ambitious set of goals for the collaborative network, with a move away from a notion of joint planning towards simply informing one another of developments.

Negotiation

There was clearly a relationship between the negotiation process initiated at the assessment stage and the development of collaborative networks. In fact, it was the process of negotiation which provided important clues about network partnerships and the way they revolved not just around the fairly innocuous idea of working together but of doing so in a context of real differences and tensions which might drive them apart. This was because negotiation reflected both the wish to work together and the difficulty in doing so. In many cases, these tensions and the consequent complexity of the negotiations were connected with issues related to risk and compulsion. As far as the practitioners were concerned, the presence of risk made it much more likely that thought would be given to developing a negotiating strategy.

Certain ways of conducting negotiations, particularly those concerned with risk, were seen as more successful than others. For example, there was frequent reference to the need for 'network conferences' as a way of overcoming barriers to effective decision making.

Relationship work

One feature of the diaries was the way references to relationship work crept into descriptions in ways which indicated that it was seen as a basic assumption rather than an explicit focus of the work. However, one practitioner explicitly linked quality of support to quality of relationships and another linked the establishment of trust and a certain level of personal familiarity to the whole process of inter-agency work.

While it was clear that practitioners were concerned with maintaining the networks they had helped to develop, it was not clear how much attention was specifically given to the support needs of those involved. There was some evidence of the importance attached to enabling support to be accessed, for example, by putting people in touch with support groups. But the extent to which professionals saw their own role as a supportive one in relation to anything other than direct work with clients was not clear.

Interestingly, where the issues were of a more managerial nature and not linked to the welfare of specific individuals, there was likely to be a more explicit focus on the quality of the links between members of the network. In this sort of network considerable attention was given not just to issues such as good communication but also to the overall development of relationships and mutual support.

Summary

In this chapter, we have begun to look at the results of our direct work with community care practitioners. In particular, we have focused on the record of collaborative work contained in the community care diaries that the practitioners' group were asked to keep. One issue that emerged was that many of the practitioners seemed to operate two very different approaches to community care assessment. The co-existence of these service-led and collaborative models led us to describe the situation we found as 'between two cultures'.

Overall, certain themes seemed to influence everything else:

- A sensitivity to and a willingness to respond to the demands of a particular situation.
- Personal credibility.

and

- Attention to communication processes.

These emerged strongly once again in the course of the discussion groups which are the focus of the next chapter.

4 Discussion and reflection

Themes and questions

The next step in our work with the practitioners was to discuss with them some of the implications of what they had written in their diaries. This chapter is concerned with what came out of our meetings. To protect the confidentiality so important in a small project like this one, a commitment was given not to include quotes or to identify individuals. We have respected this while trying to convey a flavour of the discussions.

Altogether, we held three discussion groups. Over the course of these discussions certain themes emerged about collaborative skills and their relationship to collaborative culture. In the following sections we describe these themes in the context of the topics around which they clustered. We begin with assessment as a collaborative activity.

The assessment process

Open minds and open systems

During the very first of the discussion groups, it emerged clearly that assessment was frequently seen as a collaborative activity. Moreover, this group suggested that relationships established at the assessment stage would very often form the context for all subsequent decision making. The word used to describe collaboration in defining need and planning support was 'openness'. The assessment system was seen as open not just in the sense that it involved talking to several different people, but also because it was rooted in a value system which became quite explicit during the course of the group discussion.

A nurse related openness to the holistic or 'whole person' approach – the need to relate to all aspects of a person's life and to see the connections rather than to be narrowly focused on illness or specific problems. A social worker related openness to the principle of choice, that is the importance of obtaining as much information as possible to enable the service user to make meaningful choices.

The difference in terminology and emphasis reflected differences in professional culture but what was more striking was the complementarity of these values. Subsequent discussion groups confirmed this link between an inter-disciplinary orientation towards openness and commitment to collaborative work. Certainly the practitioners themselves had no difficulty in understanding one another's values and philosophies or relating them to collaborative practices.

Building relationships

All of the discussion groups acknowledged that early on it was not always easy for practitioners to find ways of working with one another or with service users and carers. In so far as a collaborative approach to assessment was seen as hingeing on a process of engagement with others, it was agreed that a key strategy was the development of relationships over a period of time. While, in social work in particular, there is a long tradition of focusing on relationships with service users as a part of the assessment process, it is not always recognized how important the process of relationship building is in relation to the collaborative network as a whole. This point was picked up and developed in the groups.

During the first group, it was emphasized that 'engagement' encompassed relationships between professional groupings and between agencies. In this way, it was stressed, liaison and inter-agency work contributed to the development of the kind of relationships which would make collaborative forms of assessment possible.

Task-based roles

It was during the second group discussion that someone emphasized the importance both of collective decision making in the planning process and the need for clarity about who was doing what. On the face of it, this seemed puzzling. But as discussion progressed it became clear that an important paradox was involved. What was described as 'blurring of role boundaries' had to go hand in hand with what was described as 'clarity about roles' and it was the group that first described this paradox which offered a resolution of it.

The key seemed to be the relationship between 'blurring' and 'clarity' on the one hand and 'coordination' on the other. What was suggested was that if there is a sufficiently high level of collective responsibility and collective identity, then the consequent blurring of role boundaries would lead to a more informed awareness of where there were real differences in knowledge and skill and a greater ability to make constructive use of them in the work. What was being suggested was, in fact, the need for a move away from stereotypical thinking about roles of the kind exemplified in statements such as:

'because I am a district nurse / social worker I will do this'

or

'because you are a district nurse / social worker, you will do that'.

Instead it was being argued that roles should be linked to a shared understanding of the actual knowledge and skills available to a collaborative network and their relevance to a unique set of circumstances.

As a way of building up shared understandings about knowledge and skills, a social work manager specifically recommended 'shadowing' other practitioners to get a better understanding of the nature of their work; an idea picked up with some enthusiasm by others both in this and subsequent group discussions.

Sharing assessment means sharing power and feeling empowered

The opening up of the assessment and planning process to others was mostly seen as an extension of, rather than a challenge to, professional identity. In other words, there was a noticeable absence of defensiveness on the part of these practitioners about their own expertise. It was acknowledged that this might not be universally true and that where practitioners feel oppressed by their managers they are less likely to undertake the kind of power sharing necessary to the establishment of collaborative modes of assessment.

One person in the first group suggested that even where there was some collaboration with other professions, those practitioners who did not feel empowered by their managers would be unlikely to share power with service users and carers. Other members of the group agreed that to share power we need to feel empowered ourselves. To some extent this turned

conventional wisdom on its head. Professionalism is often seen as antago-
nistic to empowerment. But here, professional autonomy and a self-confi-
dence were linked to, and even to some extent became prerequisites for,
collaboration.

But even if there is a commitment to sharing power and to collaborating
with others in an assessment, all three groups felt that certain key skills
were needed in order to make these things happen. In particular, it was felt
that individual practitioners and managers needed to be skilled communi-
cators, able to adapt their style to a wide range of different circumstances
and people. If the groups were engaged in the process of defining a new
kind of professionalism, then this was clearly a major component of it.

Responsibility, accountability and assessment

In the second group both a nurse and a social worker said there was a need
to recognize that some practitioners had very specific responsibilities and
accountabilities which could not simply be negotiated away. This point
seemed to support the more general observation that cooperation is likely
to be enhanced by a realistic understanding of the concerns and responsibilities of others. Simplistic solutions based on a denial of the facts are not
helpful.

During the third group discussion the theme of professional responsibility and its relationship to the assessment process was developed in a new
direction. A social worker argued very strongly that one way of exercising
professional responsibility was to make a decision as to the most appropriate way to assess a situation. She also pointed out the significance of context. If a referral was made in the context of a ward-round at a hospital it
would almost inevitably lead to a multi-disciplinary assessment, whereas if
it were made in the social work office or by telephone, then there would
need to be more of a choice made.

This highlighted the difference between those collaborative relationships
which are constructed on the basis of lack of clarity about responsibility
and those which are made as a result of some strategic decision to involve
others. It also made it clear that a strategic decision to collaborate is not an
abdication of professional responsibility. Rather, it involves a complex series of judgements about who to approach, how to approach them and
what their role should be in relation to the assessment process.

Multiple perspectives

The third discussion group saw a social worker arguing for the key importance of two factors: 'respect' for the views / knowledge / expertise of others, combined with an awareness of the importance of ensuring that there is

some level of integration so that services can be delivered in a rational and appropriate way. In making these points she was pointing to a key dilemma about collaboration – how to facilitate and empower others to say what they think, while ensuring that the efforts of the collaborative network are coordinated effectively.

In fact, in discussion it was recognized that a plurality of views can strengthen rather than weaken the collective effort. Different perspectives may represent different aspects of the truth and, just as important, different kinds of needs which have to be addressed in the collective decision-making process. To take a different approach and to seek to ignore awkward opinions is likely to lead to the breakdown of the collaborative network at some future date.

Power sharing

As far as the first group were concerned power sharing, especially with service users and carers, was something which all of them took for granted, in the sense that they saw it as a routine part of their practice. They saw power sharing as involving two key areas of skill – flexibility and the ability and willingness to share information. A nurse pointed out that being in the community as opposed to an institution was in itself a source of power, while a social worker highlighted one specific empowering strategy, which was to make management aware of the problems being created for service users and carers by lack of resources.

During the second group discussion, the relationship between power sharing and negotiation was explored in more detail. It was suggested that service users had the power to refuse both services and ways of working and this would include the power to reject a collaborative networking approach. A social worker suggested that the use of feedback to inform service users and carers was an empowering strategy. The social work manager pointed out that the new procedures, such as the incorporation of self-assessment into the assessment process, were giving service users more influence than before.

This discussion left us with a sense of frustration. In spite of an obvious commitment to empowerment, or at the very least 'responding to the wishes' of those they worked with, the practitioners found it difficult to identify key issues for practice; and there was almost no reference to the way in which power was manifested in their own relationships with service users and carers. In theory, service users might, for example, have the power to reject services or styles of service delivery, but in practice they might well accept what they were offered for fear of the consequences. We concluded that a more grounded and realistic discussion about this would be likely to take place during the planned workshop, when service users and carers as well as practitioners would be present.

Coordination and the mobilization of resources

The way in which this topic was explored in the groups was in terms of a number of more specific issues.

Regular contact

On the question of coordination and mobilization of resources, all the groups agreed that this was an integral aspect of their role as community care practitioners and stressed the importance of regular contact with those with whom they were working. In general there was a commitment to a team approach.

Strategies

Over the course of the group discussions, a number of specific strategies were mentioned as ways of ensuring that resources were effectively mobilized and coordinated.

Ensuring that regular meetings take place between practitioners, carers and service users was mentioned by a nurse, as was the importance of following up arrangements and checking on progress.

One social worker explicitly linked liaison with mobilizing and coordinating resources. She emphasized the importance of prior knowledge of other agencies and an established liaison relationship with them. This also led her to include developing trust and the 'nurturing' of relationships as coordinative skills.

All the groups agreed that poor relationships between health authorities and social services departments hampered their own efforts to mobilize and coordinate resources.

The question of lead responsibility

One issue which emerged in the first and second group discussions particularly strongly was that the practitioners did not always assume that they should be the ones responsible for coordination. But it was also clear that this decision had less to do with professional expertise as such than with the way in which practitioners became involved. If they took lead responsibility early on in the development of a piece of work, this would gradually tend to translate itself into assuming responsibility for overall coordination. If another practitioner took on this lead role, even if the situation were very similar, they would tend to leave coordination to them. This practice might change with the full introduction of new care management practices, but nevertheless drew our attention to the link between roles and processes.

Leadership, trust and clarity

During the third discussion a social worker raised an issue which appeared to be linked to the tricky question of leadership. She felt coordination required someone to have a clear vision of the kind of things that needed to happen. She also emphasized that collaboration should not be an excuse for dumping responsibilities on to others. Trust was important and could only be built if people were frank and honest. She also pointed out that persuading people to get involved in these kinds of collaborative work practices was not easy.

Through discussion certain things were identified as critical ingredients of trust. These included clarity about the nature of the work: not suggesting, for example, that it was simpler or less demanding than it really was, and trying to spell out in a realistic way some of the implications. This was particularly important when working with service users and carers. Clarity about the kind of collaboration envisaged was also critical. It was recognized that there was scope for considerable misunderstanding about roles and relationships and that this kind of misunderstanding could undermine trust. Finally, there was the intangible but vital question of personal credibility. The way one had conducted oneself in the past would always have consequences in the present and the way one conducted oneself in the present would be bound to impact on future relationships. This emphasized how important the time dimension is in this and other aspects of collaborative work, which is always a product of its own history.

Close working relationships as an alternative to coordination

The second discussion group drew attention to the relationship between certain ways of working and the teamwork which was so central to community care philosophy. A nurse said her own experience of the 'care programme approach' had been very positive. This involved identifying a core group of practitioners who would work closely together. In her view this provided the right kind of environment for collaborative practices to develop. She also emphasized the value of joint working, including joint visits to service users with other professionals. There was some general discussion about this which showed that it was not only beneficial to give some thought to ways of focusing collaborative energies most effectively, but that where there was a sense of being part of an integrated whole the need for day-to-day coordination might be less. In other words, where people were working closely together, coordination – in the sense of explicit management of the work – was unnecessary.

Liaison and coordination

Some of the difficulties that could arise when trying to mobilize resources from other agencies were discussed in all the groups. During the second group discussion, a social work manager and a social worker both independently stressed the importance of liaison in establishing an atmosphere in which other agencies were responsive to requests for services. Emergencies posed particular problems, they felt, because one would not be able to route communication through those individuals one already knew. One solution to some of these problems, they suggested, was to establish closer inter-agency relationships by working towards a 'shared set of objectives'.

The management of conflict

The groups constantly returned to the theme of conflict and how it might best be managed in a collaborative framework. They focused on this broad area of concern in a number of particular ways.

Conflict and the negotiating process

Issues concerning negotiation and the management of conflict became linked in our discussions. It was generally recognized that where there was actual or potential conflict, negotiating skills played a key role in maintaining and developing the partnership network. During the course of the first discussion group, a social worker suggested that some conflicts could be prevented if attention were paid to possibly contentious issues, such as confidentiality and finance, at an early stage. On the other hand, she also felt that good practice could lead to conflict, as when taking on an advocacy role in relation to another agency. This raised the interesting point that professional consensus should not be bought at the price of 'selling out' the interests of service users. In other words an ability to negotiate on the basis of an explicit conflict was preferable to collusion and, moreover, compatible with a commitment to partnership and collaboration.

The second discussion group emphasized the importance of an ability to negotiate one's way out of overt conflict and out of situations where everything seems very 'stuck'. A social worker argued that negotiating skills were particularly important when there was ambivalence on the part of one or more key players in a situation. The group discussed this and concluded that ambivalence often reflects covert conflict and in turn makes it difficult to generate effective commitment to goals which have apparently been agreed.

Establishing or re-establishing the conditions for collaboration under such circumstances was seen as essential but very challenging. One rule which seemed to emerge from the second group discussion was that where either overt or covert conflict is identified, it needs to be addressed straight away before it gets worse. This was a point made by a number of people but put particularly strongly by a social work manager.

Honesty and working with conflict

Working with conflict is a value-driven activity. In the second discussion group, working with conflict was explicitly linked to a concept of honesty by both a nurse and a social worker. By honesty these practitioners meant something more than simply telling the truth. Through discussion, the group as a whole decided that honesty meant a willingness to confront difficult and possibly conflict-ridden issues directly with those whose trust and confidence was essential to the success of collaborative work.

Honesty involves being able to explore the difficult and conflict-ridden situations which can arise in collaborative work. In particular, the second group made the point that it is very important to be able to make explicit the different perceptions, values or interests which might lie behind conflicts with other professionals or with relatives and carers.

Collective responses to conflict

One issue stressed by a social worker in the second group was the way in which the whole of the collaborative network needs to play a part in resolving differences and conflicts between different members. This was picked up by the group as a whole and developed. Racism was singled out by a nurse as an area of conflict which needed to be resolved collectively, even if it initially seemed to involve only one or two people, and the group as a whole seemed to agree.

This notion of collective responsibility for conflict resolution created some new dilemmas, when it was translated into practice. During the third discussion group, a social worker agreed with it in principle and felt she herself had some responsibility, but was also very unsure when it would be appropriate to intervene in someone else's conflict. This may therefore be one of those principles which people find easy to affirm as a general rule but find much harder to put into practice in a particular situation.

Support

Although it had not always emerged very clearly from the diaries, there was unanimity in all the discussion groups about the centrality of support to collaborative work.

In the first discussion group some very specific one-to-one forms of support were mentioned, like helping other professionals to cope with death and dying. But the main emphasis was on more general ways of offering support to carers and professional colleagues, which included both emotional support and practical support. In relation to the latter, it was suggested that one key aspect of being supportive was being responsive to requests for help – the implication being that bureaucratic delay was incompatible with a supportive stance.

During the second group discussion, the participants suggested that one small but important ingredient of support was simply recognizing the contributions of others. A social worker felt this was often forgotten by professionals in their dealings with one another. She argued that positively valuing one's own supportive work and being prepared to set time aside for it was vital. A nurse added that listening to people when they wanted to offload their feelings was important and helped them to feel valued.

In the final discussion group the importance of offering support to carers by making time for them was emphasized. A social worker said she often made specific visits to talk to carers rather than trying to see them at the same time as service users.

Network conferences

Here it is important to give space to something which emerged very strongly in the second discussion group and which does not fit neatly into any one topic area. This is the central place of network conferences in what could be described as 'strategic thinking' in relation to support, conflict resolution and empowerment.

As a strategy for support

As a support strategy, the group emphasized the value of network conferences as part of the professional support system. A social work manager emphasized the similar role played by meetings of the managers' network in which he was involved.

As a strategy for conflict resolution

In terms of conflict resolution, the group agreed network conferences were ways of enabling those holding very different views to begin to empathize with one another's perceptions. It was also suggested that by enabling all those who attended to develop a fuller understanding of differences in their points of view, conferences laid the groundwork for collective decision making which did not marginalize minority viewpoints. If conferences were to succeed as conflict resolution strategies, it was agreed by the group that it was very important to invite, and then to do everything one could to encourage, the attendance of those who may not normally attend conferences but whose views need to be acknowledged if realistic plans are to be made.

As a strategy for empowerment

The group suggested that in relation to empowerment, network conferences could be seen as strategies for increasing the power of service users and / or carers in relation to practitioners. By inviting service users and carers to participate in open processes of decision making, their own views were likely to have more weight than if decisions were made on the telephone or in private discussions between practitioners. A social worker described a practice of holding network conferences in the home of the service user rather than in an office and in this way symbolically giving some power back to them. All agreed that inviting service users and carers to attend was clearly not enough. People needed to be enabled to participate fully and if necessary to challenge the views of professionals there and then.

The organizational context of collaboration

Organizational culture

In the second and third discussion groups a set of issues emerged in relation to the organizational environment and its impact on networking and collaborative work in general.

There was clearly ambivalence about the role of management. Members of the first group recognized both positive and negative features. They suggested that the organization as a whole can be threatened by the participative, democratic characteristics of collaboration. In particular, they suggested that hierarchical organizations which place a strong emphasis on containing the flow of information and the processes of decision making within very circumscribed limits can react very negatively to attempts to develop a networking approach. On the other hand, they also saw their organizations as recognizing networking as a way of becoming more effective by creating more and better opportunities for communication and innovation.

The general organizational culture seemed to be the key factor. The group members felt that the most network-friendly organizations were those which could be described as 'task cultures', whereas those which were least network-friendly were more traditional 'role cultures' (Handy, 1981), in which the preoccupation with maintaining power and control led to attempts to reduce or confine the scope of collaboration. All the practitioners were clear about what they wanted from their organizations. They wanted management to set guidelines or frameworks within which they could feel free to operate, but not to interfere with their day-to-day collaborative work.

Access to organizational resources

The second and third discussion groups also focused on that aspect of the organizational environment which related to the scarcity of resources, including resources for networking. All those involved felt that decisions about priorities affected what they were able to do. There was considerable uncertainty about the rationale for these decisions. It seemed to us that this kind of uncertainty was likely to demotivate staff and possibly act as an obstacle to creativity and initiative. Collaboration plainly required good communication between management and those working directly with service users and carers.

Networking

All the groups were asked to think about the process of developing collaborative networks and, based on their own experiences, the following ideas or definitions emerged:

- Working together towards a common goal, with each person contributing something different.
- Creating a web with a common thread so that all the parts are linked together as a whole, dependent on one another.
- User involvement, shared understanding and contacting people at the right moment.
- Communication, discussion and coordination with various service

providers and users and carers, and the mobilization of resources to address assessed needs in terms of a common goal.
- Inter-agency and intra-agency work.
- A process of partnership in assessment.

Putting all these suggestions together we came up with the following definition of the skills involved in developing collaborative networks:

Helping to create some kind of purposeful pattern or 'web' of communication and cooperation based on the acknowledgement of difference.

This concept of the 'web of communication and cooperation' seems to us to embody a very powerful image of collaboration. It draws attention to both the complexity and the strength of the links that bind individuals, groups and organizations together and emphasizes that while there may be many different kinds of strands they are all equally important and all bound together in a strong and purposeful design.

Education and training for collaboration

Finally we asked participants to think about their own and other's training needs in relation to collaboration.

The message that came through very clearly from the first two discussions was that there was a need to overcome the lack of understanding that different professionals and different agencies had of one another's roles and areas of expertise. At least one practitioner also felt there should be courses available for carers as well as for practitioners. Two specific expectations were mentioned.

First, there should be opportunities for mutual sharing and learning. Second, there should be opportunities for developing a common set of aims and objectives for community care. Neither of these suggested a conventional academic course, and the specific training methods mentioned echoed this need for dialogue rather than instruction. One idea was discussion groups for nurses, social workers and others, perhaps including carers. Another idea was shadowing other practitioners in their workplace situations.

While these comments might indicate an entirely informal and workplace-centred approach, a social worker involved in the final discussion raised doubts about whether this would be sufficient when she pointed to the need for 'structure' and some guarantee of quality and 'common standards'.

Summary

In this chapter, we have focused on the practitioners' discussion groups. The message of these groups was clear. Collaboration is linked to an approach which recognizes that needs can only be met by a range of people working together. It is characterized by a commitment to the idea of exploring a range of possibilities and options for change with those, including service users, most closely involved in any given situation.

It seems to require an ability to involve others, particularly carers and service users, in processes of decision making; to communicate appropriately and effectively; to make good assessments drawing on a range of perspectives; to negotiate shared understandings; to manage conflict; to effectively mobilize resources and to be able to give and receive support. In terms of training, the strongest demand seemed to be for multi-disciplinary training, with a strong preference for informal discussion over more formal approaches such as lectures.

What is striking about these findings is the very large area of common ground that appears to exist between nurses and social workers and between mental health specialists and specialists concerned with ageing. There is certainly strong support here for a shared collaboration culture to underpin this type of work. In the next chapter we turn to the perspectives of service users and carers.

5 Collaborating with service users and carers

The context for service users and carers

Now is a good time for action to involve and collaborate with service users and carers in community care. The community care reforms provide a catalyst, but a number of other developments also offer a strong basis for reform. These include the growing interest expressed by government in consumer involvement in public services; the new legal requirements for consultation, comment and complaints procedures in community care; and the emergence of powerful movements of disabled people and other recipients of community care services demanding more say and involvement in policy, provision and legislation.

All of this has raised the profile of user involvement in community care planning and provision. Carers, service users and their organizations have become involved in many different ways. People are becoming more involved in their own personal dealings with community care services: for example, by attending meetings affecting them; seeing records kept about them; and making use of complaints procedures. Service users are getting involved in managing existing services and in planning and developing new ones. There are now a growing number of examples of service users being involved in community care planning, standard setting and quality assurance, monitoring and evaluation, staff recruitment and training, designing and placing contracts and running their own user-led services.

However, both service users and carers question how much real say they have achieved in community care. The gains from getting involved are generally limited, while the effort entailed is usually considerable. The consultative forums and committees and the market research exercises which have mushroomed in recent years, and which are the main expressions of

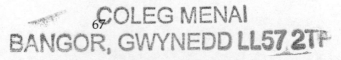

user involvement, are distanced from most people's day-to-day experience of community care practice and services. Their outcomes are also uncertain. Spending constraints seem to have exercised a much more powerful influence on policy and services.

So far service users and carers have not often been asked what skills they think practitioners need to work with them. They may be asked their views of plans, policies and services, but not of the practitioner skills which are at the heart of their experience of community care. Yet who is in a better position to say? This is a question which has guided us both in writing this book and in undertaking the project which informs it. For us a vital logic underpins it. If agencies want to work in a collaborative way with service users and carers, they will need to collaborate with them to find out how best to do so.

User involvement in training

Perhaps the nearest that service users and carers have so far come to being involved in developing skills for community care has been through their involvement in training for professionals. This involvement takes several forms. It includes service users offering contributions to courses, acting as trainers, providing their own training courses for professionals and producing training materials (Keville, 1992, p. 13; Beresford, 1994).

Clearly training, including in-service training, qualifying and post-qualifying training, is crucial in developing and implementing more participatory and empowering practice in community care (Beresford and Croft, 1993b), and the involvement of service users is central to such training. Yet so far user involvement in community care training is limited and patchy.

It is still much more likely to mean service users or carers offering a one-off slot as outside speakers than being an integrated part of learning. One group of social work students said:

> 'We've had a limited number of service users. It tends to be isolated people coming in saying "I'm disabled" and not many and not really linked. ... It's tokenism to say what disability is' (Beresford, 1994).

Service users place considerable emphasis on their involvement in training as a means of changing the culture of professional practice. In practice, it is still mostly used to offer an additional perspective to complement the conventional professional ones. So while user involvement in training is likely to have major implications for professional skills, this issue remains undeveloped.

The involvement of service users and carers in identifying skills

Policy makers, educators and service providers have so far paid little attention to the contribution service users and carers can make to the identification of appropriate skills for community care practitioners. Service users and carers are not often involved in defining the skills that are needed for agency practice and management. Little systematic attempt seems to have been made to explore this with them. Yet it is a particularly appropriate area of activity for both groups at this crucial stage in the development of community care. This is because of:

- The fundamental changes now taking place in the aims and organization of community care and community care professionals.
- The new priority attached to the perspectives of service users and carers in community care.
- The changed funding arrangements for community care and increased emphasis on budgeting and cost-effectiveness.

Community care service users and their organizations have long urged the need to work 'with' rather than 'on' or 'for' people. A growing body of evidence is emerging from them which highlights the kinds of approaches to the provision of support which they value and prefer. This builds on:

- The development by disabled people of a social model of disability to replace individual and medical models.
- The new emphasis from disabled people's organizations on people's rights as well as their needs.
- The development by disabled people of self-run personal assistance schemes and user-led services.

Colin Barnes highlights the importance of involving service users in the definition of both people's needs and practitioners' skills in his discussion of disabled people and discrimination. He shows that historically 'professionals" perceptions of need are frequently at odds with those defined by disabled people and their organizations and that 'disputes between disabled people and professionals over the form and levels of service considered appropriate are not uncommon'. He concludes that:

Comprehensive assessments of disabled people and their families by professionals remain central to the process of service allocation, and professional power within welfare bureaucracies continues to go unchallenged (Barnes, 1991, pp. 133, 147).

As service users and carers have increasingly expressed their views and a start has been made to seek their views, a growing amount of evidence has emerged that service users' views of health and social services do not necessarily match the professional view (Siddiqui, 1993, p. 13). One study showed that when patients and nurses at a psychiatric hospital were asked which aspects of care they rated most highly, the two groups had very different perceptions. For example:

> Patients rated 'drug treatment' and 'being seen at ward rounds or case confer-ences' in their bottom four items. Nurses placed these in their top four (Sharma, 1992, pp. 20–21).

Involving service users and carers in developing skills

Two key points emerge from all this for the involvement of service users and carers in developing skills for community care. First, service users and carers are likely to have some mould-breaking things to say about skills for community care. Second, because little has so far been done to explore this, any attempt to do so will have to break new ground. We realized that we would have to start from scratch in the project. But while there is little to build on as far as service users' and carers' views about community care skills are concerned, there is now considerable experience, information and guidance on good practice for involving people to be drawn on.

Not only would involving service users and carers in developing com-munity care skills be new for us. We could expect it to be new for them! We couldn't assume that they would be used to thinking or talking about skills for community care because, as we have seen, it is not something service users or carers have been encouraged to do. Instead the expectation has been that people are the recipients of practice rather than the active partner in or initiator of it.

The emphasis in this part of the project was on developing a collabora-tive process which offered service users and carers an opportunity to con-tribute their views on what skills are needed for community care' practice. We didn't assume that they would be in a position to discuss what a collaborative practice would or should look like, since, as we have said, this is unlikely to be a discussion most would be familiar with or be able to contribute to on equal terms. The kind of concepts upon which community care is based, like needs and needs-led, commissioning and user involve-ment, may not be ones which most service users are familiar with or with which they structure their experience. Some of the older people we spoke to, for example, weren't sure whether they had any experience of community care services because they weren't sure what these were. Our objective was for the project to provide the opportunity for a discussion about skills and collaboration on people's *own* terms. The aim was that this discussion would offer a variety of insights on collaboration, including insights on:

- What skills service users and carers identify for community care.
- What skills service users and carers think practitioners need to work in a collaborative way with them.
- What skills service users and carers think practitioners need to collaborate with service users' and carers' organizations.

This discussion would be of value in its own right, offering service users and carers an opportunity to express and develop their perspectives on skills for community care. It would also be of value in making comparisons with what practitioners said.

Carrying out the project

We carried out the project by organizing a series of group discussions with service users and carers locally. We contacted service users' and carers' groups in the area in order to set up the discussions. We wanted to ask people about the kind of skills which they found helpful and unhelpful from their own experience, how they experienced their relationships with practitioners and what skills they thought would be supportive for working in more collaborative and participatory ways.

There were five stages to this work:

1 Desk research on existing information on users' and carers' views of skills and collaboration in community care.
2 Identifying users' and carers' organizations and groups in the area.
3 Making contact with users' and carers' groups, explaining the aims of the project and seeking their involvement.
4 Preparing a schedule for use in discussions with users' and carers' groups.
5 Undertaking the discussions, tape recording and transcribing them.

We also identified two additional issues which we wanted to address. The first was ensuring the effective participation of black carers and service users. Our experience suggested that specific efforts might need to be made to ensure this happened. The second issue arose from our recognition that there tend to be fewer user groups of older people – one of the groups we were focusing on in the project than other groups of community care service users. Because of this it might be necessary to bring some older people together specifically for the project. In the event this was not necessary because there was an active organization of older people in the area, but this is unlikely to be the case in all areas.

We carried out seven group discussions. These were with:

- Users of a daytime service for people with mental distress.
- Two carers' groups in different parts of the area.
- A group of older Asian women, with caring responsibilities.
- Disabled people involved in an organization of disabled people, which included older disabled people.
- Members of a self-advocacy organization of people with mental distress.
- Members of a forum of older people.

We made efforts to involve as diverse a range of groups as possible in a small-scale project. The groups included people who came together as users of a service, people involved in service user self-advocacy groups, people involved in a group with a paid worker and people involved in carers' groups concerned both with offering mutual support and influencing community care policy and practice.

We gave the groups both verbal and written information about the project before the discussions were held. At the discussions, we made clear commitments about confidentiality and feedback and permission was sought and obtained for tape recording and transcription of discussions. All the discussions were recorded and fully transcribed in this way.

We developed a flexible schedule for use in the discussions, drawing on our contact with the groups before carrying out the discussions. The core areas to be covered included:

- People's experience of community care services.
- People's attitudes to community care services.
- The skills they felt service providers need to meet their individual needs as service users and carers.
- The skills they felt service providers need to work with users' and carers' groups.
- Their ideas and suggestions on how these skills might be developed.
- What, if any, problems they saw in working as a group with community care agencies and workers.
- The skills they felt they need as a) individuals and b) a group to work effectively with community care services.

- The relation of skills in community care to other essentials for effective and sensitive services.

The schedule was flexible so that members of groups could introduce particular issues that concerned them and extend discussions about particular areas covered as they wished. We told all the groups about the second phase of the project, where it was planned that service users, carers and workers would have a chance to meet together, exchange views and develop discussion. All the groups expressed an interest in taking part in this meeting.

What people said

The findings from this part of the project confirmed the value and importance of involving service users and carers in the process of identifying and developing skills for community care. Their views did not necessarily reflect professional expectations and assumptions about what is important for service users and carers. Participants seemed to welcome this chance to offer their views and emphasized the importance of exploring ways of accessing what they said to practitioners and policy makers at local level and beyond.

They had things to say about skills and collaboration whether they were experienced members of users' and carers' groups or individuals whose only contact with services was as users of them. The only difference there seems to be between the two is that the latter often have more difficulty in formulating proposals and demands and would benefit from more support in developing their views and ideas.

People's experience of community care

The people involved in the service users' and carers' groups had between them experience of a very wide range of community care practitioners and services. These included community nurse, home help, community psychiatric nurse, physiotherapist, general practitioner, social worker, community transport and occupational therapist, as well as home chiropody service, day centre, day hospital and counselling service. They didn't only mention designated community care services and practitioners. One carer, for example, spoke of a policewoman who was very helpful to his wife who had a drink problem.

The range of services and practitioners, and the variety of agencies and authorities responsible for them, could lead to problems of coordination:

'The health authority says it's the local authority. The local authority says it's the county authority. The county authority says it's the health authority, so you go round in circles. No one has a pot of money to pay for it really. It's also true that there are a great many different types of organization at different levels, some of whom are competing to provide these social services ... There is a bewildering number of organizations related to doing something in mental health' (Local self-advocacy organization of people with mental distress).

Cuts in one service could result in another collapsing:

'We have one member who has support from a variety of different people, different groups and the one thing she had which wasn't covered by anybody else was a home help who used to come in and do her washing. That was withdrawn because it wasn't an "essential task", but in fact the washing had been done, including all the bandages because she has ulcerated sores, which meant that when the district nurse came along twice a week to replace her dressings there weren't any clean bandages. So from the council's point of view, washing isn't essential. From the health district's it's nothing to do with them. But taking the two services together, if you withdrew one, the other collapsed. So they actually replaced that service. They reinstated it' (Local organization of disabled people).

People reported problems of access to services. As some carers said: 'You don't know the right people to contact, do you?' For the group of older Asian women, the problem was not that they didn't know how to contact services, or what services there were, but actually *getting* services. Increasing charges are also restricting access to services:

'Social workers do not charge, but you need to pay for home help. I used to pay £2.50 per hour. But these days the charges are so high it is better to hire a private one' (Group of older Asian women).

Service users' and carers' experience of community care services and practice was very mixed, both as individuals and as a group. They could never be sure what kind of treatment they would receive or how helpful a practitioner would be. People talked about good and bad experiences and about workers they regarded as really helpful and poor:

'And when you think back, you can't think back sufficiently to get a clear picture of what you went through. It's a nightmare' (Local carers' group).

'Sometimes the home helps can be erratic and not come' (Local organization of older people).

'The social worker was such a source of help to me. I couldn't have done without her' (Local carers' group).

'My neighbour had a home help service every day and a district nurse twice a day. And I would highly recommend what happened with him until he died ... He had marvellous attention' (Local organization of older people).

Attitudes to community care

As a result, people's attitudes to community care practice and provision were mixed, ranging from 'My experience? Diabolical, in just one word' (Local carers' group) to:

'I have found them extremely helpful ... a very, very positive experience' (Local self-advocacy organization of people with mental distress).

'A good professional worker can make all the difference' (Local carers' group).

Clearly service users and carers found some professional practice unhelpful rather than helpful, for example, when unrealistic commitments are made:

'Hospitals promise you the earth. "Oh yes, take them home. That will be fine." This person will be in, that person will be in, and you wait and eventually you cope and you don't bother and they don't turn up and they don't bother' (Local carers' group).

They also expressed a sense that professionals often don't have the appropriate skills:

'Health workers aren't provided with the skills and language to consider people as people ... Workers are stalled from seeing other ways of helping people by the narrowness of their experience and training' (Organization of disabled people).

'They just go by the book. I would say that my doctor, my psychiatrist and my experience of hospitals have all gone by the book ... I went back to my doctor and told her I was very angry with her. She said, "Oh why?" and I said because I needed your help and your only answer was to put me in touch with the duty psychiatrist at the hospital who wanted to admit me. And her answer was she was told I should have been admitted' (Local self-advocacy organization of people with mental distress).

Skills for a collaborative approach to community care

It was when service users and carers discussed skills for community care that it became most apparent how different their world-view was from that of the service system. If anything emphasizes the importance of involving service users and carers in the definition and development of skills, it is this. It doesn't necessarily mean that their views are in conflict with those conventionally expressed by community care agencies, services, trainers or practitioners. Rather they tended to see things differently – to have different starting points, to frame their ideas differently and perhaps to have different conceptions of what constituted skills.

People's comments and trains of thought didn't always fit neatly with our initial terms of reference, so it was important to be flexible. They raised new themes and issues. Some individuals and groups found it difficult to discuss some of the issues we raised. In order to do justice to the breadth of people's thoughts and ideas it may be helpful first to headline separately the different responses of service users and carers to the key areas we explored, before going on to look at some of these in more detail. Let's begin with the carers' discussions.

The skills carers identified

The skills workers need to work with individual carers

- Patience.
- Understanding and empathy: 'If you've got a very ill patient who is unable to assert themselves … they can be pushed around a lot.'
- Experience – workers need to know what caring is really like.
- The ability to 'really listen'. If workers listen to what carers say they won't make judgements about them.
- To have information to pass on to carers: 'You need someone with knowledge of where you can get help.'

The skills needed by professionals to work with carers' groups

- Experience or understanding of caring, illness and disability.
- Information and knowledge about local services, benefits, finances, disability and different illnesses.
- The ability not to make judgements or assumptions about people.
- The ability to communicate with each other.

The skills carers' groups need in order to work effectively with community care services

- To be well organized.
- To be clear about what you want.
- To be able to put in writing what you want.
- To be able to maintain your independence as an organization.
- Assertiveness.
- To know the terminology and legislation.

- To be able to think positively at a time when there are not enough services and resources to meet your needs.

Additional issues raised by carers

- Carers have to work very hard.
- Caring affects every aspect of people's lives.
- People may not choose to be a carer.
- Often when you start caring you do not know where to get help.
- Even if you do know where to go to get support, you may find there are not enough services: 'I cared for something like 16 years for my mum without any help.' Some people can't get any help at all.
- Sometimes the services that exist can be very unhelpful for carers. You may have to be very assertive to deal with services.
- Carers really value having a social worker of their own who can help them.

Older Asian women's group discussion

The group of older Asian women did not see themselves as a group either of service users or carers and did not come together on that basis. But they had experience both of providing and receiving support. Their particular experience of community care meant that their response was different from that of the other groups of carers and service users.

- Many women in the group had problems and difficulties that meant that they really needed support. They would like help from community care services.
- The women knew what services there were and how to contact them, but when they contacted social services they were told that because of cuts in services no help was available. They had to struggle on without help.
- It was difficult for women to comment on how services could be made better for them when they had little access to services in the first place.

The skills service users identified

Now let's turn to what service users said about skills for community care.

The skills service providers need to work with service users

- The ability to treat people with respect as individuals.

- Being able to provide information.
- The ability to listen to what people say.
- Communication skills.
- Being able to help people identify their needs instead of acting as gatekeepers.
- Good networking between services.
- Well-publicized services.

The skills service providers need to work with service user groups

- Able to take groups seriously and value them.
- Able to take part in joint discussions with service users' groups.
- Able to develop consultation skills.
- Able to back up groups.
- Able to tell other service users about the groups so they can get involved.
- Able to recognize the discrimination service users face.
- Able to involve service users in training professionals.
- Able to train disabled people as community care workers.
- Able to recognize users' groups' needs for resources.
- Able to provide appropriate information.

The skills users' groups need to work well with community care professionals

- Confidence.
- The ability to work in a professional manner: for example, to take minutes accurately, to be able to handle meetings.
- A realistic approach to what's possible.
- Able to put criticisms positively.
- Able to provide appropriate information.
- Able to work with other community organizations.
- Training.

Additional issues raised by service users

- The need for adequate resources.
- The need for enough time to make change.
- The need for more people in users' groups. This is linked to resource issues, such as travelling expenses.
- The need for more support services run by voluntary organizations.
- The need for service users and workers to be involved in joint discussions.

Issues service users and carers raised about community care skills

While the philosophy of this project was based on involving service users and carers, we were also careful to distinguish between the two. It is important not to confuse one with the other, for they have different perspectives, interests, rights and concerns. Carers have often been used to speak for service users, and this still happens. While this project provided opportunities at all stages for each group to speak for itself and offer its own different account, one of the interesting issues to emerge was how similar – in kind if not in detail – service users' and carers' concerns were about collaboration and skills for community care. We can see this through the three groups of skills that have been identified: those for practitioners to work with individual service users and carers, those to work with their organizations, and those for service users and carers to work with community care practitioners and agencies.

Skills for working with individual carers and service users

Service users and carers identified a wide range of skills which they felt were needed. There was considerable agreement between the different groups about these skills. They included seeing the individual as a whole person, not as a set of symptoms or problems; treating people as individuals, not as an anonymous group or class; treating people with respect; acknowledging the validity of their experience and views; providing them with full and accessible information; listening to what they say and asking them what they want; recognizing the need to meet them on their own terms and if possible on their own ground, where they would feel more comfortable and relaxed:

'I think perhaps [there is a need for] more of an understanding of old people, to listen more carefully to them' (Local organization of older people).

'I think a lot of it is basic consideration for people … It is treating people as individuals. Treat them as humans. It's all that sort of thing' (Self-advocacy organization of people with mental distress).

'A simple example. Jane has arthritis and is partially sighted. She is 62. In social services' terms, because of the way the teams are all split up, is she an older person or is she somebody with a sight impairment or is she someone with a mobility impairment? And because the teams are all split up into various groups, it gives you a view that people are split up into these groups and the truth is we aren't!' (Local organization of disabled people).

'They've got to have good listening skills, and I mean really good listening skills because we don't always say to other people what we want to say … It takes a lot of trust to be able to tell somebody the truth about how you feel and what you really want' (Local carers' organization).

'If you could pick up a phone, phone somewhere and say something is happening, this is happening, what do I do and where can I go for help' (Local carers' organization).

Skills for working with service users' and carers' organizations

We wanted to explore the skills practitioners need to work collaboratively both with individual service users and carers and with their organizations. There were many overlaps in the skills people identified for effective collaboration in both situations. This was particularly true of the carers' groups, where people placed an emphasis on many of the same skills. The skills people highlighted included: providing information, confidence-building, knowledge of resources, listening and having a commitment to service users' and carers' rights, needs and interests:

'People who have time to talk, listen – these are the basic things' (Self-advocacy organization of people with mental distress).

'I thought they needed to listen to what the carer thinks he or she needs: information on what's available in the area such as volunteers, respite care, home helps; not to impose their views on clients – let us say what we want; and to give information on financial matters … and we need regular visits from the social worker … it must be a definite commitment to come at that time' (Local carers' group).

A common concern among people who took part in the discussions was the importance of both health and social services taking them *seriously*. There were real worries and fears about tokenism, based on some people's experience. Service users and carers stressed the need to support groups which were independent and under their own control to become established, and then once they were, for practitioners and services actually to listen to what they said and recognize and respond to their continuing need for resources. Such a commitment was seen as essential for effective collaborative working. It was felt to be reflected in consulting people and groups *before* decisions were made rather than afterwards:

'I think the main [skill] is to take the group seriously … I mean they promised me the CPNs [community psychiatric nurses] will send people along [to the group]; different things are going to happen, but it never happened … It really annoys you because I'm doing it all and I'm on the helpline and I say anybody can ring me anytime. You don't want praise for it, but you want some back-up' (Self-advocacy organization of people with mental distress).

'To really communicate with us and other groups and by doing that to develop their consultation skills. ... We're trying to get them to consult us *before* they do things' (Self-advocacy organization of people with mental distress).

'Consultation is a rubbishing word because half the time they've already made up their mind what they're going to do and then they consult you after the act and this is what's happening' (Organization of older people).

Skills for service users and carers to work in collaboration with community care agencies

Service users and carers identified a wide range of skills which they found helpful in working with agencies and professionals. These covered three main areas: skills for personal development, technical competencies and skills for organizing. Mostly these could be gained by experience, by agencies ensuring that accessible information was available and by enhancing people's confidence. One group highlighted the importance of their members' technical skills, which facilitated their effective dealings with health and social services organizations, skills which they felt meant they were highly competent and professional. These skills included being able to provide detailed and accurate minutes, undertake important negotiations and produce businesslike correspondence.

At the same time there was a feeling that service providers should recognize that some groups might not have these skills and that collaboration should not always demand them. Service providers should be sensitive to working in ways which are comfortable for service users' and carers' groups and not expect them to be the mirror-image of other professional groupings. This requires new skills from service providers, both in being sensitive to different ways of doing things and in adopting these different ways themselves in their dealings with service users' and carers' groups:

'We need assertiveness. We need to know the terminology. You have to know the legislation and how the various organizations, shall we say the statutory authorities, interpret the legislation' (Local carers' organization).

'Confidence ... What you do need to have is an effective group of people who've got the confidence to basically deal with professionals ... We've been lucky in the way this group's developed. We've got people with skills like that and people with different skills we've been able to use. We've got the best minute secretary ever' (Self-advocacy organization of people with mental distress).

It was clear from the comments of some of the groups that working with community care agencies could be a difficult, demanding and painful experience. Members of one group said:

'You also have to be practical and realize you can't change the world ... It does take a lot of time to change things ... you've got to have your life as well' (Local organization of disabled people).

All these skills may be needed at a time when people are going through considerable difficulties, with inadequate material and personal support. Some service users and carers seemed to feel a lack of support from practitioners at both a personal level and as members of groups. The kind of skills which they mentioned needing in their personal dealings with services, like assertiveness and being clear about what they wanted, might also be seen as a measure of the shortcomings of professional community care skills.

Summary

In this chapter we have begun to look at what service users and carers had to say in the development project about skills for community care. One of the interesting findings that emerged is how often skills and values which might be expected to be taken for granted in qualified practitioners are lacking in their experience. Because of this, service users and carers placed a particular premium on such qualities as respect, reliability and openness. There were some important overlaps here with what practitioners said. Another significant finding was the high degree of similarity between what service users and carers said. The different perspectives, interests and rights of these groups are rightly stressed. But their overlaps and shared concerns, as this emphasizes, are no less important.

6 Raising the concerns of service users and carers

Concerns expressed by service users and carers

In addressing the questions we raised about skills and collaboration in community care, service users and carers also identified a number of other related issues which concerned them. They reflect the context of collaboration as well as some of the boundaries that currently limit it. They also open up the discussion beyond conventional professional parameters. It will be helpful to look at these concerns next.

The relationship of skills for community care and professional and organizational cultures

Service users and carers made a number of references to organizational cultures and traditional professional cultures which were not consistent with more collaborative and participatory approaches to practice in community care. They highlighted that skills for collaboration in community care need to be seen in the broader context of professional cultures and philosophies and that these cultures may need to change, if such skills are to be effectively adopted and developed. Training in new skills on its own would be unlikely to be effective. It needed to be coupled with changes in attitude. Members of the local organization of disabled people said:

'I think in the seventies people were beginning to open up to ideas that maybe people had some sort of right to what was common experience, and isolating and controlling people wasn't the way forward. But you get vast differences in attitudes. Because, for example, if you go to a hospital and talk to hospital people, they're much more into telling you what you can do and what you can't do and treating you very much as a patient. If you go to social services, you're more likely to bump into someone who is talking to you as a person about what you want to do and how, how you can achieve it and how you can take responsibility.'

Issues of resources and agency culture

The problem of inadequate community care resources, cuts in agency services and budgets were common themes in the discussion. For instance:

'Can we get it absolutely clear from the start that local authorities are providing the services with the resources that are available to them. If more money was coming from central government into localities, more could be done!' (Local organization of older people).

There was an understanding among participants that inadequate resources would limit the nature and quality of services available to them. For them it meant a limit on how often and how long they could see a practitioner, restricted opening hours for valued services and not enough of the services they wanted. They called for increased funding and resources. But while this was seen as important, it was not seen as the only problem. Resources were coupled with an appropriate culture for more empowering and collaborative working. There needed to be change in *both* if community care policy and practice were to be needs-led. There are both resource issues and skills issues; both must be addressed and they need to be given equal priority. Limited resources don't prevent cultural change, even if they may inhibit it. For example:

'There are still resources that social services can call on. There are still innovations that social workers and care managers and so on can bring about. They can be a lot more imaginative in the way they use resources' (Local organization of disabled people).

Different agency responses to self-help and self-advocacy groups

Service users and carers had experience of collective involvement in groups that were concerned with offering mutual support, and in groups concerned with expressing a users' or carers' voice, by offering users' or carers' views and providing feedback to service providers. Some groups serve both purposes. Some are more specifically concerned with the provision of self-help support. One discussion group felt that with the increasing emphasis on user involvement, there was beginning to be some recognition and understanding of the needs and role of self-advocacy groups, with some earmarked funding for them, but that service providers were still often less clear about those of support and self-help groups. As a result, these could be left unsupported to 'get on with the job', imposing a great strain on their members. Service users and carers thought a good understanding of the aims and needs of such groups would helpful for more collaborative working:

'I think we're getting two kinds of groups and I think there are important differences. This group is a consumer feedback group ... It is politically fashionable for all government services at the moment to show that they are paying attention to customers: and so the hospital gave us money because they wanted us to do that ... but there are a lot of groups who try to provide a kind of social service – a drop-in centre, a therapeutic centre, a meeting centre – that get nothing at all from social services' (Self-advocacy organization of people with mental distress).

At the same time, groups which are primarily concerned with representing the views of their members and working for change are also increasingly conscious of the need to offer their members support. While self-advocacy groups are trying to draw together the two strands of self-help and action for change, agencies still seem to be drawing a distinction between them. As we have seen, getting involved can be a demanding and stressful experience, particularly for people who are experiencing difficulties. So while groups may have a different emphasis, all are likely to have some concern with providing support, and this needs to be recognized by community care agencies and practitioners. This has implications for skill development to enable practitioners both to be sensitive to and able to support the diversity and changing forms and objectives of self-organizations.

Differences between health and social services

Service users and carers talked about both similarities and differences between health and social services. One difference that was identified with implications for a more collaborative approach to community care was the emphasis on a medical model in health. Some service users found this unhelpful and inconsistent with their equal participation. Such differences in culture and philosophy are likely to have an important bearing on the different learning needs of workers in these two services:

'I think another area that is a problem is health workers. We're saying there's a difference in attitude. Health workers in their training aren't provided with the skills and language to consider people as people. They consider people as patients and cases, so that then they're stalled from seeing other ways of helping people by the narrowness of their experience and training ... In social services, you're more likely to bump into someone who is talking to you as a person ... They speak totally different languages' (Local organization of disabled people).

Reconciling the skills for an interpersonal approach with the new budgeting and purchaser arrangements in social services

The new arrangements for community care will have profound implications for the role and skills of social workers and other social services workers. Care managers will be expected to put together care packages, understand budgets and possibly manage them, as well as making assessments which are needs- rather than service-led. Service users attached considerable importance to social services workers having the skills to negotiate and operate this new care culture effectively.

Training which was centrally concerned with a traditional interpersonal approach to social work would not necessarily offer this. As a result, social workers could be disempowered and ineffective when seeking to deal with the new system. Ultimately this would be detrimental to the interests of service users and carers. They felt there was an urgent need for social services staff to gain the new skills now required if service users' and carers' needs are to be appropriately met:

> '... If you imagine being a social worker is a game, they've been trained and run to the game rules. Now they're having another set of rules imposed on them ... Most people aren't trained and even their experience of life which has led them into training isn't to do with budget control, resource control, breaking the bad news to people that they're not going to get what they need ... There's been a great change and very few of them have got experience of management of change, to learn how to cope with radical rethinks' (Local organization of disabled people).

Community care services must be accessible for people to be involved in them

The group of older Asian women weren't getting the services they needed and wanted. Discussion about what skills were needed was undermined by the fact that they did not get a service at all. If they were referred by their general practitioner to a social worker, the social worker frequently did not come. Because women did not get a service, they did not feel it was their responsibility to identify skills. The problem was not lack of knowledge about where to get services, but not being able to get them when they went:

> 'People say that social workers help out, but I have been ill for the last seven years, no social worker ever came to see me. Even my GP wrote to the social worker but still nobody came round.'

> 'From time to time officers come to this group and explain to us about the social services, but usually social workers do not help out.'

'It's up to you how you improve these services.'

This group highlighted a vicious circle which affects black people and members of minority ethnic communities more generally. Because they don't receive community care services, or services are inappropriate, they are less likely to be included as part of the discussion to change those services and less likely to see it as something they should be part of. Where this happens, practice and services are likely to develop in a way further and further away from meeting their rights and needs. Because of this it is important to adopt a *pro-active* approach to practice, which encourages practitioners to explore local patterns of needs, instead of a *reactive* approach, based on responding to whatever needs have traditionally come forward.

Training for service users and carers as well as service providers

Service users and carers highlighted the need for the development of new skills among community care practitioners and managers. For example:

'The local authority is closing down a home with 50 people in it. Practitioners need information on how those people can live in the community, like, "What do we do? Who do we contact? Where might funding be available?"' (Local organization of disabled people).

However, they didn't see training needs stopping with service providers. They felt that it was important that resources for training were not solely directed towards professional training. They also identified the need for training for service users and carers and their organizations if they were to collaborate with community care and other services on more equal terms. These included training to increase people's confidence, assertiveness and expectations. Several groups placed an emphasis on confidence-building. Confidence was regarded as important both for individuals as service users and carers and when they were involved in service users' and carers' organizations interacting with providers of community care. As people said, when you are using such services you are likely to be particularly vulnerable and stressed. Your confidence may be at its lowest. Confidence-building is therefore essential:

'Special training in skills, like, for example, going to college and within that college you would be seconded to various organizations ... The reason is because that person could be faced with certain situations and not everybody could handle it' (Users of a daytime service for people with mental distress).

Service users and carers also thought training was needed to develop practical skills. These included skills in communicating, advocacy, resource management, planning, negotiating and dealing with official agencies, as well as knowing where to go to get information, learning how to work together in groups and developing their own ways of doing things. Equal opportunities training was also required, including disability equality and anti-racism training.

The centrality of general practitioners

The comments of service users and carers confirmed the centrality of general practitioners (GPs) in community care, as primary service providers, budget holders and crucial agents for referral. For most people, they were the pivotal figure in their relationship with services. They are the community care profession which people are most likely to be in routine contact with and they have a high profile in the community. Among the large group of older people who took part in the project, they were the service most people had made use of. Yet GPs have been the profession least involved in collaborative developments around the community care reforms.

Their central role in community care puts a particular premium on the development of collaborative skills in the initial and subsequent training of GPs, although there may be many problems in the way of this:

'I found my GP, my mother's GP, hasn't been at all helpful. He more or less wiped his hands of it.'

'My experience is quite the opposite. When John got ill like this, the first thing my GP, who's a wonderful person – a woman – said was you must go to social services and I wouldn't have known about this group or anything other than from my GP in the first place' (Local carers' group).

'I found his attitude very dismissive. I know he's got a lot of people to see and I didn't come out with a particularly good feeling. When I saw the CPN (the community psychiatric nurse), the CPN was a lot better' (Users of a daytime service for people with mental distress).

'You've got to be in the system … And if you haven't got a very good GP and if you're not very vocal and you're not as capable as you were, then you don't get into the system and you're left floundering' (Local carers' group).

Issues arising from service users and carers

One of the aims of this project was to enable service users and carers to speak for themselves about skills and collaboration in community care. They were certainly able to do this. Much of what they said may be familiar to practitioners who seek to work closely alongside service users and carers and their organizations. It may be less familiar and more challenging where traditional, more paternalistic approaches to practice and learning persist. It is not our intention to offer a commentary on what service users and carers said or place our own interpretation on it. But we do want to single out for reflection some key issues which emerge from what they said.

The importance of experience

Service users and carers placed great weight on their first-hand experience. Crucial qualities which they believed practitioners needed to offer appropriate support were the understanding and empathy which came from such experience. While they argued the value of first-hand experience, they did not say it was essential. What many did feel was important, was that where practitioners did not have such experience, they were prepared to learn about it directly from service users and carers. So, for example:

> 'What I am saying is for social workers to be in contact with us, to know what we are experiencing ... Each one of us, although we're the same, each of us has different problems and it's only by talking to us that the social workers can understand and go on from there' (Local carers' group).

Their approach to skills was not based on a crude notion that common-sense experience was everything, but instead seemed to follow from a developing theory which prioritized people's understanding, feelings and subjectivity and which sought to comprehend the nature and detail of those. This might mean a psychiatrist really listening to a service user's experience, or a social worker staying for a length of time with the woman whose husband had Alzheimer's disease and hit people with his walking stick, 'and seen him and had a whack with the stick'.

Service users and carers saw two ways in which skills for collaboration could be developed – through experience and through training. Some placed most emphasis on experience. Some saw training which drew on their experience, and which helped practitioners gain insights into that experience, as offering the way forward:

> '... By involving professionals and carers together in training. We got to understand each other very well. And I think they began to understand some of our

problems, you know, by the training and the little group work' (Local carers' group).

The interrelation of skills and values

Service users and carers were not just concerned with technical skills, although there seems to be an increasing emphasis on them in community care training and they thought they were important. Carers, for example, wanted practitioners to have a grasp of the kind of practicalities that concerned them, like lifting, forms of medication, and so on.

Service users and carers did not place any emphasis on skills in terms of specific skills for particular areas of practice: for instance, in assessment, review or matching services to individuals. It was as though something more important had to precede this. This was workers' adoption and internalizing of a particular kind of value system and culture in relation to service users and carers. At the heart of this was an explicit valuing of service users and carers.

Service users and carers seemed to have realistic and reasonable expectations of workers. They were generally tolerant of their shortcomings, mistakes and failings. What they were less likely to excuse was being kept in the dark, patronized, ignored, lied to or deceived. They pointed to a different philosophy of practice. Older people stressed the need to have 'respect for old age'. Disabled people argued the importance of appropriate learning: for example, being familiar with a social model of disability.

Skills and values seemed to be closely bound up for service users and carers. What they saw as skills, others might see as values or human qualities: for example, honesty, commitment, candour, patience, tolerance, empathy and reliability – workers providing accurate information or coming when they say they will.

It may be argued that these qualities are preconditions for entry into or qualification in professional training, but the experience of service users and carers suggests that such values and skills cannot be taken for granted in practice. They often seem to be lacking and some service users think they may actually be weakened rather than strengthened by conventional professional training.

Service users and carers seemed to see changed practice values as a prerequisite for developing specific practice skills. This has important implications for a strategy to develop collaborative skills in community care. It also has parallels with the approach service users and carers have adopted in developing their own skills. Their view is that if they are to learn and use practical skills effectively, they must first value themselves and develop their own confidence, self-esteem and assertiveness (Beresford and Croft, 1993b). Similarly if practitioners are to adopt skills to work collaboratively with service users and carers, they must first learn to value service users and carers.

Challenging the legacy of training

Training has been presented as the main way in which community care practitioners can improve the way they work with service users and carers. Yet in the view of some service users and carers, professional training actually often seems to *distance* workers from the people they work with and to desensitize them to their own and other people's feelings. As a result some service users felt they were being subjected to an alien philosophy or ideology of 'care' rather than the human understanding, empathy and support – the extended human skills – which they wanted. For example:

> 'They tell you to do things without understanding why you can't do them or offering help to do them' (Self-advocacy organization of people with mental distress).

> 'I found the GP's attitude very dismissive. I know he's got a lot of people to see. I didn't come out with a particularly good feeling' (Users of service for people with mental distress).

The distance between professionals and service users has been increased by professional training and recruitment policies which have discriminated against service users. So while the service users and carers we spoke to put a high priority on first-hand experience, this has largely been seen as a minus rather than a plus for professional practice. The implementation of equal opportunities policies to recruit disabled people, psychiatric system survivors and other service users as community care educators, trainers and practitioners offers the most effective way of challenging the depersonalization of practice and the exclusion of service users' experience from it.

People's different levels of experience and involvement

People involved in the service users' and carers' groups had different backgrounds and degrees of experience in both their individual and collective dealings with community care services. This reflects the general picture. Service users and carers are likely to be at many different stages and have different levels of knowledge and expectations. Some of the people we spoke to had a very thorough understanding of the new arrangements for community care, had been involved in efforts to influence policy development, had sat on joint planning and other planning and participatory structures and had received training on community care and user involvement.

Others did not have this experience and were primarily concerned with their own situation, as well as the general need for change and improved skills if their needs were to be most appropriately met. This meant that participants in the project had very varied levels of experience and understanding of the issues under consideration. This is typified by the contributions of two members of one of the carers' groups:

> 'We now get invited to virtually anything that's going on, such as there was a discussion about a stroke rehabilitation ward and there was a seminar last Thursday and our national organization was invited to that.'

> 'My husband, he died three years ago, but he had Alzheimer's. I just didn't know what to do with him and I didn't know about Alzheimer's. I didn't know what it was and when I was with the doctor ... I said to him, what am I going to do? What shall I do now?'

There must be recognition of and value given to the differences in experience and skills which exist both within users' and carers' organizations and between them. Appropriate support should be offered to develop people's understanding and skills, if collaboration is to be effective and not tokenized.

Starting with people's personal experience and agendas

Service users and carers start with their personal agendas and experience. It is generally because of their roles as service users or carers that they become engaged with community care services. Their interest in community care begins there, although it may develop beyond this into collective action and the formulation of collective agendas and demands. Service users and carers are sometimes criticized for their 'personal agendas'. It is important to remember that community care is concerned with the provision of personal services and that people's personal experience and agendas should be valued as the necessary starting point for service provision, planning and delivery. This is not always the case and community care gets lost in organizational, managerial and other structural issues. But it needs to be taken into account both in developing skills and in collaborative working.

Learning from doing

We had two main aims in our work with service users and carers. We wanted to offer them an opportunity to be involved in the discussion about community care skills and we wanted to find out more about their views and ideas about these skills. Collaboration and involvement weren't just central issues we wanted to explore and develop in the project. They were also *essential* for carrying it out. If we were to involve service users and carers in the project on equal terms, we would have to be able to collaborate with and involve them effectively. So in its work with service users and carers the project had to draw heavily on such skills itself. This included skills for identifying people to take part in the project, to gain their cooperation, to enter into discussion with them and to maintain their involvement.

Because of this, the process of the project offers some helpful insights into the skills that are needed for collaboration, as do the findings. These reinforce what service users and carers said and adds to their picture. But again, like them in their discussions, we found it difficult to separate skills from values and other issues. Perhaps that is one of the important lessons to learn from this project: that the three are not necessarily divisible. So let's look now at some of the most important lessons that emerged for us in collaborating with service users and carers. But first perhaps we should offer a word of reassurance.

Don't be disheartened!

In this discussion, we have tried to be honest about the demands and difficulties of involving and collaborating with service users and carers. Seeing these problems set out in detail, however, may be offputting and

---

Exercise

Why should service users want to be involved?

Statutory community care services are now required to involve service users by law. Agencies are now seeking service users' involvement with more or less enthusiasm. Many seem to think this is an offer service users will find hard to refuse. Most service users do seem to turn it down though. Why should service users want to be involved? After all, it can be a lot of hard work with little to show for it. Try and think of five good reasons why you think service users should want to be involved.

Feedback

This is the kind of question which gets harder to answer the more carefully you think about it. Initially it seems a very good deal. You'll have a chance to give your views. People will know what you think. You could improve how the service works. But the reality isn't always like that and service users and carers have become increasingly aware of this from bitter experience.

intimidating. We hope not, because this is not our intention. We hope it will be much more a matter of to be forewarned is to be forearmed.

Sometimes when you read accounts of schemes to involve people, the picture is one of unqualified success, with people rushing to take part, no shortage of quotable comments and a massive enthusiasm to stay involved. The truth is usually some distance from that. First, involving people is a hard slog, as will probably already have become clear from this book. That is not because people are not interested or apathetic, or because the workers trying to involve them are necessarily doing it all wrong. Getting involved is still something out of the ordinary for most of us. That is especially so for people who have spent any length of time in the community care service system and have been segregated and disempowered.

But getting involved can be worth it – if it is made worthwhile. Ways of doing this include agencies and professionals:

- Not making decisions until service users have been involved.
- Ensuring that participatory initiatives are properly funded.
- Paying service users' expenses and a fee for their expertise.
- Making the possible outcomes of involvement clear at the outset.
- Giving weight to what service users say.
- Ensuring participation is fun as well as work.
- Giving feedback promptly to service users about what has happened as a result of their involvement.

The crucial thing to remember is that it is the service agency's and practitioner's responsibility to encourage people's involvement, not the responsibility of people to get involved.

Getting involved worries and frightens most people. They wonder, 'What will they ask me? Will I know what to say? Could I get into trouble? Will I do it all wrong?' We should remember that this is just as true for service providers as service users and carers. People have also got many other demands on their life and may be having a struggle just keeping their head above water. So don't expect a massive response and do not devalue a small one. Participation and collaboration are long-term strategies that take many small steps to come to fruition.

Involving and collaborating with people

Now we will look at some of the lessons we learned from this part of the project. They fall into three major areas, concerned with involving people, collaborating with them and ensuring the equal involvement of black people and members of minority ethnic communities. These are three areas of key concern to service users and carers. Hopefully, by setting them out in this way, we will also help readers to take these ideas forward in their own practice, through the practical insights they offer. Let's start with trying to involve people.

1   Involving people

Making contact with local service users and carers

The best way of making contact with service users and carers is through their own organizations. In some areas, there are still few user-led groups. In many, there are not user-led groups for all groups of service users, such as older people, disabled people, people with learning difficulties, mental health system survivors and so on. In those cases it is worth looking to regional or national organizations to see if they can put you in touch with local contacts. Generally there are also voluntary organizations, local umbrella organizations and some practitioners who are in touch with individual service users and carers, if not groups, who may be able to provide a starting point.

Ours was a local project. We used several methods to identify and reach service users and carers and would recommend trying as many as possible. They pointed to the value of community development skills in such work. They also highlighted the importance of finding out about and making use of existing information. The methods we used to make contact with people included:

- Drawing on the knowledge of the local authority social services department training officer who was involved in the project.
- Referring to existing information and guides, such as that produced by the social services department about local groups.
- Making contact with people involved in local community care networks.
- Finding out about local service users' groups from people with more general knowledge of service user networks.
- Snowballing – which simply means finding out about other contacts as you go along from those you have already made. It was in this way, through the coordinator of the day service for recipients of mental health services, that contact was made with the self-advocacy organization of people with mental distress.
- Finding out more about local minority ethnic communities by networking with members of these communities, with whom we were already in touch.

Such contacts represent a valuable asset. They are there to be built on for further work, as well as helping to ensure that as wide a range of people as possible can become involved.

Clarifying the terms of involvement

We made careful efforts to explain fully to people the terms on which we were seeking their involvement. When this happens people know what they are taking on and can make an informed judgement about whether they want to be involved. We explained the aims and nature of the process, who was undertaking it and who was funding it. We explained that the project was independent of the local authority and local services. Equally it had no power to effect change in local services. The aim was to bring together people's ideas and experience which would then be available to be fed into local and national discussions, hopefully to influence policy and practice.

We also made clear that strict confidentiality would be observed in the project. No one would be identified by name, unless they wished to be, and what individuals said in groups would remain anonymous and confidential. Groups would not be identified by name without their agreement. People were asked for their permission for discussions to be taped and transcribed. The issue of confidentiality was emphasized to the transcriber. People were promised that they would be kept in touch with what happened.

Starting with groups

Efforts to gain people's views tend to be based on individual interviews or group discussions. We opted for group discussions. We did this because in our experience they ensure greater equality in the relationship, by increasing people's confidence and assertiveness. They ensure a wide range of views and experience, and help discussion to develop as participants interact with each other.

We also thought it was important to involve service users and carers who were involved in existing groups. We did this for two reasons. First, while such groups are often criticized by service providers as 'unrepresentative', they are generally democratically constituted organizations which have clear links to the service users' and carers' movements. Second, such groups have played a central part in the development of service users' and carers' thinking and action and havealready been widely involved in debates about community care.

Individual service users and carers may have limited opportunities to reflect on and make sense of their experience of community care. They may feel they should be grateful for whatever they get. They may not know what else might be possible. While they may have worries and reservations about the way they are treated and the service they receive from community care, they may be reluctant to criticize it and not know how it might be different. People in this position need time and support to think through their feelings about services.

Being involved in a group can make a real difference to individual service users and carers. It means that there are opportunities for people to think through, reflect, discuss, exchange and analyse their thoughts and feelings. This is one of the strengths of the user movement and one of the reasons that people involved find it supportive. You discover how your experience relates to others and find out that your concerns are not strange or remarkable, but shared by other people too. You begin to feel less isolated and more able to work out and express your views. It is important that efforts to involve service users and carers should build on rather than bypass or ignore this experience.

2 Collaboration

Providing information

When carers' and users' groups are asked for their help, they need information in clear and straightforward terms so that they have a good idea of what is being asked of them. They generally have very limited resources and many demands on their time. People want to be able to make judgements about whether it is worthwhile to get involved. Generally groups involved in this project wanted information on paper so that they could discuss it with each other informally, or at a meeting. In one case, we made an initial visit to explain the project in more detail, as well as sending information. A small poster was made and put up in the day service for people with mental distress to let people know about the project. In all cases there was discussion on the phone, and information was again given as clearly as possible when we met members of the group.

The importance of sensitivity

Service users and carers are not another set of professionals to be coopted into the traditional community care process. Collaboration means practitioners and services making a cultural shift to include service users and carers, not them having to learn the way practitioners and services work. This means being sensitive to their needs, rights, preferences and concerns. Meet people on *their* terms, in their territory. Recognize their generosity in giving their time, both as individuals and as a group. Try to fit in with their arrangements. Use language which is accessible, appropriate and not patronizing. Ensure information is provided in accessible formats and meeting places are fully accessible. In our project, for example, some of the discussions were held in the evening. All were held where people wanted them to be held. Some had to fit in with other business that the group needed to discuss, or in one case with people having their lunch.

Where agencies and practitioners are not sure how best to respond appropriately to service users and carers, it is best just to ask. Service users and carers also value acknowledgement of their effort. As they say when it has not happened: 'It costs nothing to say thank you.' As we have said, groups and individuals are at different stages and levels of development. There is no one user or carer voice. All have important things to say. Sensitivity will improve the chances of them all being included and of them all wanting to take part.

Encouraging people to develop their own agendas

Practitioners and service agencies should not expect people to have the same agendas as them, or to be familiar with the issues which they think are important. People know most about their own experience. Often that means their direct experience of services. That is what is important and familiar to them. They will want to talk about their own personal dealings with services and to begin with may find it difficult to talk about more abstract or wider issues.

It was to accommodate this that we used a flexible, semi-structured schedule, with a relatively small number of open-ended questions, and made it clear to participants that they could include what they wanted to in the discussion. People's experience is the heart of the matter. They may have few chances to talk about it, least of all with people involved with community care, so it is important to ensure that they have that opportunity. It is also valuable in its own right and provides vital insights for broader practice and policy issues.

Developing trust

Trust is a prerequisite for effective and enduring collaboration. Agencies and practitioners have to develop a track record of collaboration. Service users' and carers' groups are often cautious, and understandably so. Their experience of user involvement in community care has frequently been negative. Consultations often do not lead to much. It is not often there is a history of positive partnership with community care agencies. Trust is something that practitioners must work to foster and gain. It cannot be taken for granted. Why should service users or carers trust professionals or services? Do not take it personally if they have reservations.

One of us is a service user. This is important for building trust with service users and enabling their involvement. Service users should be involved in the development of any initiative for collaboration or participation right from the start. Trust can also be gained by being clear about what you want; making limited demands on the limited resources of service users; making clear what gains, if any, there may be for them; and making sure they are fully and quickly recompensed for any expenses they incur.

Group work skills

Group work skills are at a premium in the kind of discussions which our work with service users and carers required. Discussion groups may be small or large. Each requires a different approach and different skills. The smallest discussion in this project was with three people, the largest with more than 50. They were very different, but equally valuable. It is important to value small as well as large discussions. There are many obstacles in the way of people getting involved in such discussions. There are practical problems, like lack of time and opportunity. Many people are also worried or frightened by the idea of taking part in a discussion. It is necessary to ensure that people have a sense of support to encourage them to take part and offer their comments if they want to, without them being placed under any obligation or pressure to participate.

Collaboration takes time and effort

Collaboration is exciting and rewarding, but it is not an easy option. It demands time and effort as well as skill. However much effort and time you expect it to take, it is likely to take more. This is one of the lessons that managers and service providers seem to find hardest to learn.

The discussions which we organized for this project lasted from between half an hour to about an hour and a half. But they all took a lot more time to set up. People needed to have the chance to discuss the idea at a meeting. Groups needed to fit them into their schedule. This is an important part of the process and cannot be rushed. The people we met with were generally very busy, with limited resources, as well as often having other constraints on their time.

Collaboration has to fit in with service users' and carers' timescales and priorities. These are people who are likely to be under pressure, under-resourced and quite probably without paid workers. Groups may meet monthly or perhaps less often. They have to keep their members informed. What time they have together is precious. Making contact is likely to mean a lot of cold calling, which requires confidence and being clear about what you are doing. Keeping in touch with them is likely to mean a pattern of making numerous phone calls, listening to answerphone messages and having to call back again. Groups may want an initial meeting with the practitioner or agency to sound them out, check out what they think of them and make a group decision. You may have to make a one-off journey, wait while they go through the rest of their agenda and then have just a few minutes to explain what you want. It may feel frustrating. You may feel irritated, especially if you have to do it more than once, but this is what collaboration means if it is to be real rather than rhetorical. It is also a token of the respect which people have a right to expect and another expression of the increasing assertiveness of service users.

Feeding back to people

We undertook to send service users' and carers' groups a copy of the final report of the project when it was produced. We are sending them a copy of this book. We also explained about the second stage planned for the project, which we discuss in the next chapter, when anyone who wished to could come to a meeting where they would meet other service users, carers and practitioners involved in the project. We saw this as an important part of the feedback process. There they would have a chance to learn more about what other people had said and to take forward the discussion together. This project confirmed other experience that participants in such projects greatly value being kept in touch. If you contribute to something, you want to know what has happened and particularly how much notice has been taken of your views and ideas. Letting people you have involved know what is happening is important. It does not matter if there is not much to report, or the news is not good. People want to know what is happening. Otherwise they are unlikely to get involved again.

3   Involving black people and members of minority ethnic communities

Large numbers of people from minority ethnic communities, particularly people from Asian communities, live in the area where the project was located. There is much evidence to suggest that black people and members of other minority ethnic groups are under-represented as users of community care support services. Concern has frequently been raised about the degree to which such services match the needs of minority ethnic communities (Baxter and others, 1990; McCalman, 1990; Gunaratnam, 1992). Ensuring the involvement of black people and members of other minority ethnic groups was identified as a key concern in the first national survey of user involvement in social services (Croft and Beresford, 1990). Unless specific efforts are made to involve them, all the signs are that they will be inadequately represented in schemes to consult and involve people.

We expected that this would be the case in this project. In the event, while some members of minority ethnic communities took part in the discussions, they did not reflect the numbers of such groups living locally. Members of the discussion groups were predominantly white. For this reason, we made specific additional efforts to involve members of minority communities, particularly members of local Asian communities.

One member of the project team made contact with a local radio station for members of local Asian communities, to pursue the idea of a phone-in to provide wide access for members of Asian communities. It was not possible to pursue this idea because there was no clear response from the station.

We also made contact with a local Asian women's project. One of the groups which met there was a group of older Asian women. With the support of the project and the agreement of the women, a discussion for this project was held at one of their regular meetings. They requested that the facilitator should be a woman and that the discussion should be in Punjabi. Here the help and skills of the translation and interpretation unit of the local authority were invaluable. A woman worker from the unit acted as interpreter at the discussion and the unit then transcribed the discussion into English.

The interpreter spent an hour before the discussion with the English speaking worker from this project, running through the schedule and discussing how to undertake the session. The Punjabi speaker would have liked more preparation time. We had modified the schedule for use in this discussion. Although we had sought to be sensitive to the culture of participants, some of the issues did not make sense to them. It was clear that concepts like 'service user' and 'carer' were not ones with which the women were familiar. It also appeared that members of the group might fall into both categories, while not necessarily seeing themselves as in either.

The inclusion of the group of older Asian women ensured that views from some members of local Asian communities were included in the project, although clearly we should like to have extended this involvement of local minority ethnic communities. It also highlighted the importance of not imposing assumptions about community care and the provision of support upon such groups.

We also made provision to ensure that members of the older Asian women's group could take part in the get-together meeting. The interpreter was again available. She had been briefed so that she would translate the flip charts for Punjabi speakers and interpret during the meeting.

The issues which were raised in this project about the involvement of black people and members of other minority ethnic communities raise in microcosm the broader issues relating to their involvement and partnership in community care. Major issues emerge about the need for additional funding and support both for specific black and other minority ethnic groups to be able to get together and for service users' and carers' groups in general to be able to reach out effectively to involve minority ethnic communities fully.

Summary

This chapter has explored some of the broader concerns about community care expressed by service users and carers in the development project. Many issues for collaborative practice emerge from this discussion, both from what service users and carers said and also from the process and practicalities of involving them. The two are closely interrelated. An inadequate process of participation will qualify what people can say as well as placing restrictions on who is in a position to say something. Once people are admitted to the discussion, their different perspective mean that the terms of the debate are likely to be changed.

Service users' and carers' comments place further emphasis on the interactive nature of collaboration. Collaboration requires understanding, change and new skills from *all* participants. All need support and training to make this possible. It is about much more than changing services and practice. It is also about changing our relationship with them.

7 Putting it all together: the get-together meeting

From participation to collaboration

So what can we learn from the project so far? Service users, carers and practitioners were all interested in a collaborative way of working. They were all willing and able to take part in discussing and developing skills for community care. They all had a contribution to make in defining them. But so far these had been separate discussions. While there were important overlaps in what each group said, they had all taken place in isolation.

There had not actually been any collaboration so far, except between us and them. It is one thing to have separate conversations, quite another for there to be a dialogue. Some large questions still hung in the air. Were people's different perspectives reconcilable? Would service users, carers and practitioners be able to talk to each other? Would any agreement be possible? The get-together meeting we planned could provide some answers. It would offer an opportunity for collaboration, a chance to see how well it worked and, hopefully, coming out of the collaboration of service users, carers and practitioners, there would be information on the skills required for community care.

We did have some experience to build on. Two recent projects, in which one of us had been involved, explored related areas. These were:

- *The User Centred Services Project*, which through a series of workshops explored how service users and service providers could 'build bridges' to work together, identifying a range of skills and approaches that could be helpful (User Centred Services Group, 1993).
- *The Towards Managing User-Led Services Project*, which explored a range of issues and skills associated with the involvement of service users

103

alongside service providers in managing user-led services (Begum and Gillespie-Sells, 1994).

While these did not have the same focus on skills for community care as our project, both were concerned with:

- Drawing on the experience and ideas of service users.
- Developing collaboration between service users and providers.
- Increasing the involvement of service users in community care services.

They offered a helpful basis for the meeting. We started with two aims:

- To feed back, discuss and share ideas and experience within and between the groups of service users, carers and practitioners.
- To try to take discussion about skills for community care forward by enabling the different perspectives of service users, carers and practitioners to come together to explore and define them.

In the event we added an additional aim for the day. During the course of the project, there were signs that there was some local interest in the project beyond the people and groups who were directly involved. Some people in the local social services asked to be kept in touch with what was happening. Others told us about other activities which were taking place locally to involve and consult service users and carers. These were important reminders of the local context of the project and of the fact that not only might its findings be useful locally, but that in the local setting they could also be set alongside other developments and initiatives.

Because of this, we thought it would be helpful if we could find some way of feeding back information emerging from the project directly to local agencies concerned with community care. We decided that this was something we could do at the meeting. We invited four people with key interests in local community care to come to the last part of the meeting so they could listen to the discussion and feed it into their organizations. They offered their views, asked questions and had a chance to meet participants. The representatives were:

- The coordinator of the local association of voluntary community care organizations.
- The older people's adviser at the equal opportunities unit of the local authority.
- A service manager in the social services department responsible for providing services for older people in one part of the borough.

● The manager of the local community mental health team.

In the event all but the last of these was able to take part.

The project wasn't part of the policy formation process of the community care agencies involved. We always made this clear to participants, saying that there were no guarantees that community care agencies would take any notice of what they said. Now at least, though, these agencies would know about it.

The get-together meeting

About forty people came to the meeting. There were participants from all the discussion groups, except the older Asian women's group and the users of the day centre for people with mental distress. An interpreter was available on the day for members of the Asian women's group. They had particular problems coming because they had a meeting earlier in the day. It was agreed, however, that the proceedings of the day would be translated and reported back to them to keep them in touch and we did this. Three members of the practitioners' group were able to come. A fourth practitioner, a social worker who was interested in the project but unable to complete the diaries, also contributed to part of the discussions.

It was a lively and positive meeting. Many people spoke. It was not dominated by professionals. People seemed to enjoy it. It was informative. There were differences of opinion within as well as between service users, carers and practitioners, but the atmosphere was friendly and reflected the commitment, thoughtfulness and hard work of participants. One of the managers who came to listen to what people said commented afterwards:

'These kind of meetings are often confrontational. I've been to meetings where there are 200 people and discussion gets down to a couple of people's personal experience which nobody else is interested in. It wasn't like that today.'

We also had some contributions from people who couldn't come to the meeting. One member of the group who used the day centre for people with mental distress wrote, although she said she wouldn't be coming. She said:

'... As a follow-up to the discussion I would remark that one doesn't want sympathy but IMPORTANTLY understanding ... Instead of pumping us with tablets (creating more problems) the medical profession would do well to take TIME TO LISTEN ...'

Another woman from one of the carers' groups gave her apologies for not coming and said that she would very much like to come, but felt she was a prisoner looking after her husband. She asked if her views could be given at the meeting, which they were:

'There is no care in the community – there aren't enough resources. We don't know who to turn to for what. I battered my head against a wall for six months. Quite by accident I got on to the social worker and things became a lot easier then.'

A word about our use of language might be helpful at this point. Throughout the meeting we used the term 'skill' rather than 'competency', because we wanted to avoid terminology which might exclude some people. However, the term skill should be understood in its broadest sense as a synonym for competency, including 'knowledge' and 'values' as well as 'skill' in the narrower sense of 'ability to do things'. It was in this broader sense that service users, carers and practitioners had tended to use the word throughout the discussions we had.

The structure of the meeting

The meeting was structured in three parts. This was designed to enable participants to move comfortably from the individual discussions they had already been involved in to working together as an overall group. The three parts were:

1   Separate meetings for service users, carers and practitioners. In the meetings of service users and carers, we reported back briefly what people had said in the individual group discussions as a basis for further discussion to be shared with other groups. We asked participants to identify three or four key points they would want to raise for discussion in the large group. This was an opportunity for practitioners, carers and service users to learn what other people in their own situation had said, to share thoughts and views with them, and to begin to take their discussion forward.

It is important for people to have time on their own prior to meeting with other groups. Different groups of people need time apart as well as time together. This allows for their differences, as well as enabling people to discover similarities and overlaps. This is especially important for service users and carers whose relationships with professionals and services are often difficult and unequal. The differences between carers and service users can also be as important as those between service

users and practitioners. That is why we started the meeting with separate discussions. It provided a basis for people to go on to meet with
other groups better informed, more familiar with each other and likely
to feel more confident.

2   The three groups – service users, carers and professionals – came together, with key points from their separate discussions recorded on flip
charts. Each group briefly reported on its earlier discussions as a basis
for a general discussion.

3   The final session focused on identifying skills for community care, building on the discussions which there had already been. This was when we
would see if we could find common ground. The outside representatives were present at this part of the meeting to hear what people said
and to be available to offer any information they might need.

We will now go on to look at what came out of these linked discussions,
beginning with the first: the individual discussions of service users, carers
and practitioners.

What people said at the meeting

Part one: The individual discussions

We put flip charts up on the walls which summarized the original discussions that had been held with the service users' and carers' groups and the
older Asian women's group, for everyone to be able to see. These were read
out, like all other written material produced on the day, so it was accessible to
everyone. The written feedback for the community care professionals took
the form of handouts. The feedback was all discussed and agreed by the
groups concerned. This feedback, from service users, carers and the group of
older Asian women, can be seen in full in Chapter Five, where we use it to
provide a list of the key points these groups raised in their discussions.

The carers' discussion

The carers' discussion again reflected the way in which they placed skills in
a broader context. The issues they discussed included:

• Lack of resources, particularly the inability of social services to respond to the needs of carers.
• The unreliability of many professionals as a source of accurate information for carers.

- The fact that carers were often left to cope on their own with minimal help. This could be very frightening. It would be helpful if social services made contact every so often, to check that the carer was all right.
- The failure of professionals to communicate effectively with each another. For example, an older woman was discharged from hospital and left at home, unable to go out, because community services were not provided and friends were expected to look after her, although a case conference at the hospital had decided that services were needed.
- The lack of continuity in care between hospital and community services leading to a failure to respond to the totality of need: 'The hospitals see patients as just patients. They forget about the carers and the home. They don't see the person.'
- Long waits for patients in hospital when they are admitted.

These were the key points carers raised for general discussion:

- Workers need to know which services are no longer available as well as those that exist, if they are to provide accurate information.
- Professionals need to communicate properly with one another.
- Voluntary groups (including carers' groups) need to know how to make an alliance with the council, not necessarily a partnership, to maintain independence.
- Workers should have the skill not to assume that, because someone is a friend or a partner, s/he wants to or is able to be a carer.
- Carers need someone (from social services) who is a good listener, who has the power to act, who is an advocate, who will help them become more independent and build up their confidence.
- Carers value contact from a person in social services.
- Workers need to know what is what – all the skills that come with good communication: listening, responding, acting on information, understanding (some people cannot fill in forms, for instance).
- Carers need training to care: training in practical skills. It would help build confidence so they know what they are doing is right and do not have to learn from mistakes.
- Carers need someone they can trust – or they will not have them in their homes.
- Carers can be reluctant. The council can see caring as a cheap option.

Carers again stressed the need for skills on both sides – for both carers and practitioners. Carers also need choices, and practitioners have an important part to play both in acknowledging and enabling this. This choice ranges from choice of practitioner to being able to choose whether or not they want to be a carer. The complicated organizational structure of community care places a premium on communication skills for practitioners. Carers see an important role for suitably skilled social services practitioners.

The service users' discussion

The service users' discussion highlighted the considerable pressure they felt under both as individuals and as members of self-advocacy organizations. The issues they discussed included the following:

- Rising charges for services mean that people are having to go without them.
- The work done by home care workers has changed without discussion with service users. Instead of doing housework, which people want, they are administering medication, which they do not want them to do.
- The changes in community care have resulted in a decline in skills.
- Home care workers have been required to take on auxiliary nursing responsibilities without adequate training.
- Statutory services need to cooperate more with users' groups.
- Service users' organizations are overstretched and need more financial support.

These were the key points service users raised for general discussion:

- Many people do not go to meetings because they feel nothing comes of them – the meetings are just there to appease them.
- People do also feel they can make a difference.
- Money / resources are of central importance. If government does not provide the money, there is nothing you can do.
- But it isn't just money that's important – it is also the willingness of professionals to act on information from users' groups. Professionals are required by law to consult service users, but service users are reliant on their goodwill for action.
- There is a feeling that the purpose of the new arrangements for community care – to give priority to users' needs – has got lost along the way.
- Service users feel that the voluntary sector is the salt of the earth.

Service users felt that the community care changes had had massive effects, with major repercussions for practitioners' skills. The changes had created additional demands on practitioners and services at the same time as these were undergoing cuts. There were also changes in services and the roles and skills required of workers were changing, but without taking account of what service users say they want, either individually or in service users' groups.

Service users and carers gave equal priority to a number of issues in their separate discussions. Both emphasized the importance of cooperation and collaboration. Both identified inadequate resources as a block on appropriate services and good practice. They also restated the importance of values and basic human qualities in their definition of skills for community care. Some basic skills, which would be expected of qualified workers – for example, reliability and the provision of accurate information – could not always be taken for granted. Both offer an important reminder of the increasing involvement and centrality of service users' and carers' groups to the development of community care.

The practitioners' discussion

Let's begin with a reminder of what practitioners said. The following summary was the feedback which informed their discussion at the get-together meeting. One point which emerged when comparing diary entries with comments made in the groups was that they did not always convey the same picture. Where they were different, it was always the group or individual interviews which conveyed the picture of more positive and skilful collaborative practice. These are the issues they raised:

- Developing assessment as a collaborative activity, involving service users, carers and other professionals with different perspectives, can offer practitioners a positive alternative to defining needs themselves and then making their own response. This idea of collaboration extends to the whole decision-making process. While there may be a blurring of role boundaries, there will also be greater clarity about roles. This can be resolved by the idea of coordination: a greater collective ownership of the assessment process leads to a more informed awareness of differences within the collaborative network.
- Opening up the assessment and planning process to service users, carers and other professionals can be an extension of, rather than a challenge to, professional identity. This idea may be less developed among practitioners who feel less empowered in relation to other agencies and professionals. To share power we need to feel empowered ourselves. Flexibility and an ability to communicate with a wide range of people are essential aspects of power sharing.
- The ability to negotiate is very important in situations of conflict. It is particularly important where there are not shared values in a collabo-

rative network, resulting in difficulty in engaging people effectively and conflicts between key network members.

- Honesty is a key personal quality in resolving and exploring conflict. It is important to be straightforward and direct. Skills in facing up to conflict and being able to communicate clearly things which are difficult or painful to say are essential. Racism is an area of conflict which needs to be faced up to by everyone involved in a collaborative activity.
- Networking conferences, where people can come together to share their ideas and proposals, are an effective way of resolving conflicting perspectives on assessment and of arriving at solutions. They also empower service users by enabling them to challenge practitioners on a face-to-face basis. It is important to ensure that people who tend to avoid face-to-face interaction are encouraged to attend, as a specific way of addressing conflict within the collaborative network.
- The organization context of professional practice can both inhibit a collaborative way of working, because it is perceived as too empowering and threatening to existing hierarchies, or facilitate it, by setting limits and guidelines for action.
- Collaboration is underpinned by trust; personal relationships which grow and develop over time; and personal knowledge of a range of different services and the roles of those involved. Liaison work could help to develop the quality of relationships between practitioners and this would contribute to people's ability to mobilize and coordinate collaborative networks.
- Collaboration is especially appropriate where needs are complex and can only be met by a range of people working together. Collaboration is also linked with choice and empowerment, because it offers a way of exploring possibilities and options for change with service users. It is also linked with the need to evolve shared understandings in complex situations and, through shared understandings, develop common goals. Collaboration may need to be seen as a value, not just a method of work.
- Practitioners are better able to offer support if they are supported themselves. This support comes with shared objectives and a team approach, which involves being able to listen to and praise others. Confidentiality offers a way of making it safe to undertake more intensively supportive work with each other.
- Getting services for carers, as well as service users, is a key part of the role of practitioners. Sharing information and making skills available to carers are both ways of being supportive. To be supportive it is also necessary to be responsive.
- User involvement, good communication, shared understandings and

being able to get to the right people at the right time, are key issues for practitioners working collaboratively.

- The practice of collaboration is uneven and patchy. This is linked to what priority it receives. Developing collaborative networks takes time, and in a situation of scarce resources this leads to a debate about priorities which involves values as well as resources.
- The key training need is for multi-disciplinary training. Training methods like informal discussion are preferred to more formal methods such as lectures.
- Definitions of collaborative working include:

  - Working together with others for a common goal with each person contributing something different.
  - Creating a web with a common thread so that all the parts are linked together as a whole, dependent on one another.
  - Communication, discussion and coordination with various service providers, including service users and carers, and the mobilization of resources to address assessed needs in terms of a common goal.

A number of new points emerged and others were clarified for the first time in the practitioners' discussion at the get-together day. These included:

- Needs and service and non-service system resources vary from one locality to another. In any area, the attitudes and behaviour of key individuals, like hospital consultants, can either increase or decrease the ease with which collaborative working can be practised. The more resistance there is, the more skills are required.
- Skills in addressing anxieties and enabling others to face up to necessary risks when intervention is not appropriate are very important.
- Organizational definitions of practitioners' roles and tasks impact substantially on people's ability to act as 'key workers'.
- Handling the complexities of responsibility and accountability requires skill.
- While outcomes are often negative, practitioners can still be positive about their skills.
- The ability to work with your own feelings is a very important skill.

Building on this, practitioners raised four central areas of skills as their key points for discussion. These were:

1   Communication skills: particularly listening skills. What is a person feeling underneath? Listening to people, responding and acting.

2   Teamwork: being able to work well together with other professionals, service users and carers. Being clear about roles and tasks and who is responsible for what.
3   Conflict management: being able to work with actual and potential conflict. Addressing conflict rather than avoiding it.
4   Handling feelings: the ability to understand and manage your own feelings and to be able to think about them in a professional way.

Part two: Coming together as a group

People came together again at this stage to begin the process of discussing community care skills with one another. No attempt was made initially to focus discussion exclusively on skills issues. Instead each group was encouraged to address the issues which they wanted to. Each group, in turn, fed back the summaries of past discussions and the key issues which had been picked up so far at the meeting, so that everyone had a picture of where everyone else was.

What followed was a lively and free-ranging discussion. People expressed their feelings, and there were some strong feelings, but this took place in a friendly atmosphere of tolerance and mutual respect. It probably helped to clear the air and enabled people to work well together later on in the meeting. Service users, carers and practitioners all took an active part. These are the main issues they raised:

- It is difficult for both carers and service users to get as many people involved as they want to. They need more people to come forward. Community care agencies could help by paying service users' and carers' representatives when they take part in joint discussions, and offer alternative support to service users so that carers can be involved:

    'If carers have to spend out of their own pocket, they can't go' (Carer).

- Service users and carers both said that they need time to themselves. They cannot always be expected to use their spare time for meetings and getting involved. Practitioners and agencies need to be sensitive to this:

    'I'm just too damned tired. I just sit down in the afternoon when I don't go shopping and I'm too tired. We all need our own space. I don't think a lot of people take that into account' (Service user).

- A social worker raised the point that workers frequently have to be the bearer of bad news about what *isn't* available when what people want is services which *are* available. Social workers have no power over cuts. It takes them a long time to understand the day-to-day details of carers' responsibilities:

> 'We need to understand the frustrations of your day' (Social worker).

- Service users and carers were particularly concerned about the problem of scarce resources and this issue came to dominate the latter part of the discussion. A particular fear was that practitioners would more and more have to 'skimp' to get things done rather than be able to give them proper care and attention. One social worker spoke of demand increasing and 'a battle between quality and quantity'.

The issue of resources was a theme that ran through the whole of this project. It was raised by all three groups of participants. But it never became an excuse for not trying to think things through or make progress on skills. A number of points were made about resources:

- Resources in health and social services were inadequate.
- As well as needing more resources, people needed to work in different ways.
- The inadequacy of resources was undermining improvements in practice and provision which had developed in recent years.
- The cause of the scarcity of resources originated at central rather than local government level.
- Service users' and carers' organizations were inadequately resourced.
- Many service users and carers had to rely on an inadequate income.

Part three: Finding common ground about skills

In the final part of the meeting, when we picked up some of the themes and issues which people had raised so far, we aimed to provide the chance for people to say what skills they thought were needed for community care and for collaboration. At this stage we didn't know whether there was common ground about skills among service users, carers and practitioners. We thought there was, but each group had a different perspective and different experience. We raised the themes as three questions for the group to explore. We began with the issue of resources. We asked:

> *What are the skills needed to work effectively in a situation where resources are scarce?*

People said:

- Advocacy: speaking up on behalf of service users and carers.
- The ability to prioritize appropriately and decisively.
- Making time by managing time effectively. Holding on to fundamental issues about your role and purpose and avoiding over-bureaucratizing your work. Put contact with service users and carers first, paperwork second.
- Negotiation skills.
- The ability to make alliances with others in the struggle for resources. This is part of what it means to collaborate effectively.
- Imagination, in making the most of scarce resources and seeking alternatives.
- The ability to develop trust and invest in relationships.

The second theme which we explored was that of *communication*. The importance of good communication had been a consistent feature of the earlier discussions of all three groups – service users, carers and practitioners – and had figured in the feedback and earlier discussion at the meeting. We asked:

What is good communication and what are the key communication skills?

People said:

- Skills in listening, responding and acting – not one or two of them, but all three.
- Being able to communicate information reliably and accurately, particularly in relation to the availability and nature of resources.
- Skills in checking understanding, to ensure that communication has been effective and that what you have said has been understood.
- Avoiding ambiguity, lack of clarity or jargon in communication, so that there can be agreement among us about what is meant. Ensuring such shared meaning is important in all communication, both formal and informal, individual and collective, verbal and written, including letters, leaflets and so on.

The third theme people discussed was that of collaboration itself, and, in particular, the skills that are needed for collaboration between practitioners, service users and carers. We asked:

What makes for collaboration and what are the key skills that are needed?

People said:

- Handling yourself and other people in such a way as to demonstrate respect:

  'If they come into the house with a jumped-up attitude, my back's up. If they talk to me like a person, I'm all right. I've been down that road and I don't like it. It's about respect' (Service user).

- The ability to ensure that collaboration is based on agreed purposes, aims and goals.
- The ability to understand conflict and to maintain respect even when there are honest differences of opinion:

  'Professionals must understand conflict between users and carers. Carers feel if they are assertive, they are labelled' (Carer).

- Awareness of the potential for exploitation of carers and service users and the skill to avoid this.

The gains of getting together

If the discussions which made up the first part of this project suggested that involving service users and carers in defining skills for community care could change the nature of the debate, the get-together meeting confirmed this very clearly. Not only did all participants, service users, carers and practitioners, emphasize and endorse a new pattern of skills, they also pointed to a different understanding of the relationship between skills and resources.

Usually in discussions about community care skills, the availability of resources is either not mentioned or identified as a problem that gets in the way of practising skills as they should be practised. Here the real-life experience of service users and carers kept questions of resources at the top of the agenda. Their involvement made it necessary to relate skills to resources. This made the discussion real. It suggested ways of reconciling the crucial problem in community care of conflicts between needs and resources. So collaboration changed the terms of the debate as well as informing it.

This did not mean that the discussion was concerned with constructing skills 'down to a price' – the last thing that service users or carers would want to see – but rather pursuing skills that were consistent with an environment of short resources. This meant both skills that could be practised with scant resources and skills which would help deal with and challenge short resources.

The meeting showed that service users, carers and practitioners could talk to each other on equal terms, given a supportive, neutral setting. Collaboration *is* possible. We are not suggesting that there was not and would not be disagreement and conflict. Conflict is part of collaboration; it certainly doesn't rule it out. Collaboration can provide an opportunity to resolve conflict.

There was a surprising amount of consensus among service users, carers and practitioners about the skills needed for community care. They could work together, develop discussion and make progress. They were able to collaborate to come up with concrete proposals for community care skills and collaboration. They could collaborate to produce a set of skills which would be useful in current conditions, agree on them and share ownership of them.

The process of the meeting

The process of making it possible for this to happen, however, should not be taken for granted. How well people are able to collaborate is likely to depend on how well the process of collaboration is facilitated as well as on their own experience, skills and values. This was one of the points raised by participants, as well as a belief underpinning our approach to collaboration. We tried to reflect this in the way we organized the get-together meeting.

We wanted this meeting to be a chance for participants in the project to meet each other and to have their say. We were anxious that it should be a positive and enjoyable, informal and informative occasion. Many of the people who took part in the project had little spare time and many pressures and restrictions on them. We wanted the meeting to be a break from that, not to add to it. We therefore placed an emphasis on the *quality* of the meeting. People were welcomed when they arrived and offered a drink, and then after the first two sessions there was a half-hour break with a range of hot and cold drinks, cake and biscuits, and culturally appropriate refreshments. It was a chance to relax and to socialize. We restricted it to a half-day meeting so it would not be too long or tiring for people; they would be more likely to have time for it and be able to fit it in with other arrangements.

People spent some time in the larger group, but after initial introductions they broke up into small groups, which experience shows most people find easier to speak in. This helped break the ice and reflected the emphasis of the meeting on informal discussion. By the time the last session arrived and people were asked what skills they thought were important for working in more collaborative ways at a time of short resources, many people seemed to feel able to contribute.

We took the view that, as initiators of the meeting, we had to take responsibility for it and ensure it was as positive an experience as possible. But that is not the same as taking control of it. It is helpful to have a suggested structure and programme for the meeting, available for discussion and change. But be flexible. Do not try to predetermine what happens. In this case, a tight ship is likely to be an abandoned ship!

Running such a meeting required a range of overlapping skills. These included:

- Social skills, making it possible for a diverse group of people to feel at ease in what may be unfamiliar surroundings, with people that they may feel anxious or uncertain about.
- Group work skills, supporting people to work together and exchange and develop their views.
- Communication skills, to initiate and encourage discussion in large and small groups and to be sure that participants felt comfortable and able to participate.
- Summarizing skills, to draw together accurately what people said.
- Catering skills, to produce refreshment when it was needed.

To ensure equality at the meeting, we offered a set of ground rules at the beginning for people to discuss, amend and agree. These included:

- Using simple, accessible language without jargon or initials.
- Giving everyone a chance to speak and not interrupting people.
- The right to have a break from the meeting if and whenever people wanted to.
- Not smoking.
- Keeping what people said confidential and not raising or repeating it outside the meeting.

We were made very aware of the importance of language for effective collaboration throughout this project. Using unfamiliar language is excluding. Do not wait for people to challenge you for not being clear, even though people in service users' and carers' groups have increasingly gained the confidence to do this. Instead make a conscious effort to use clearer, simpler language. You'll still get it wrong sometimes, but service users and carers tend to be forgiving if they know practitioners and their agencies are trying to communicate on equal terms.

Language is part of wider issues of access. If information needs to be sent out in advance, it should be produced in accessible formats. Physically access should include a loop if needed for people with hearing impairments and the availability of interpretation for deaf people and members of minority ethnic groups. If flip charts are used, then it is important that the

Exercise

How can practitioners ensure that service users are involved on equal terms?

The get-together meeting raised a lot of issues for us about trying to involve people on equal terms. This is a crucial issue for any collaborative activity that involves service users and carers. User involvement is often seen as a way of helping to ensure equal opportunities by including service users and carers. But all the evidence suggests that the involvement it elicits is likely to be limited and biased, unless participatory initiatives are organized to stop this happening. Service users can expect to be in a minority in unfamiliar circumstances. This is a recipe for inequality. It is likely to be only the most confident and experienced people who come forward and even then they will probably feel at a disadvantage. Try to think of some simple ways in which practitioners and agencies can ensure that service users and carers are involved on more equal terms.

Feedback

The most common problem service users and carers report when they get involved is having their credibility questioned. Are they representative? Who do they speak for? What mandate have they got? Yet the same questions are never asked of the managers and professionals involved alongside them. The crucial starting point in working with service users and carers is for practitioners to have a friendly and positive approach and treat them with respect. There are also many other specific steps they can take to ensure they are involved on more equal terms. These include:

- The adoption of agreed ground rules for meetings to ensure equality for service users and carers.
- Outreach work to involve black people and members of minority ethnic groups.
- Always involving more than one service user or carer so that they are not isolated or tokenized.
- Providing accessible and appropriate information.
- Giving the same weight to what service users and carers say as to the views of professionals.
- Payment for the involvement of service users and carers so that they are not the only people at a meeting who are not being paid to be there.

material on them is accessible to non-readers or visually impaired participants by reading them through. The meeting seemed to work well. Participants put effort into trying to offer ideas and participate in the discussion. They talked to each other and seemed to be enjoying themselves.

Some of the reasons the get-together meeting seemed to work included the following:

- People had some investment in coming. They had already been involved in the discussion in their own groups, so the meeting meant something to them.
- Invitations to come were made throughout the course of the project – at the first group discussions, then by letter and through newsletters and by phone – so invitations were followed up.
- When people got to the meeting, they would see a face that they knew. Service users and carers had already met the people who had undertaken the discussions with them. People were welcomed and introduced to each other.
- Background information on what had happened before was readily available to put things into context.
- The brief of the meeting was quite specific – the skills needed for community care. It is easier to focus on something concrete like this, and it didn't prevent people exploring other, related issues which were of concern to them.
- The people facilitating the meeting were all experienced facilitators. They were able to be flexible, were generally able to keep calm and knew how to deal with conflict, which is essential.
- Service users, carers and practitioners were all genuinely interested in improving services and wanted to be part of positive discussions about change. They all wanted to help.
- There was money for transport and other expenses.

This is the kind of meeting which it may be very difficult to organize if your preference is for certainty! Not until the meeting itself did we know exactly who and how many people would come. Would people come at all? In the event a good number did. This was probably helped by us having made clear offers to people for support for travelling expenses, child care, respite care, and payment for lost earnings, and ensuring that we used a centrally located venue which was accessible for people who used wheelchairs. We also made sure that money was available for expenses on the day so that people would not be out of pocket for any length of time.

Meetings like this may seem unremarkable – unless they go terribly wrong. But they work well in helping people think things through, make contact with each other, gain a better understanding of their different perspectives and carry out practical collaborative tasks. But as we have already said more than once, they take a lot of time planning and preparing. It is hard work, but it can be even more rewarding. The meeting provided another example to show that service users, carers and practitioners could collaborate effectively and that there was important common ground among them about skills for community care. This provides a firm foundation to develop a practical model of collaborative practice.

Summary

This chapter has focused on the get-together meeting which brought together service users, carers and practitioners to exchange ideas and experience on the topic of skills for community care. It reports the issues which the different groups raised and describes how they were able to find common ground about the skills needed. We see how the different groups were able to work together effectively and identify skills for community care collaboratively. Guidelines are also offered for organizing such collaborative activities, drawing on the experience informing the meeting.

8 What we learned about collaboration

The collaborative process

As the project progressed, we became increasingly aware that the process of our work with service users and carers was drawing attention to issues which all agencies looking to develop collaboration will need to consider if community care is to succeed in being an empowering, responsive and needs-led enterprise rather than simply one which is oppressive, reactive and solely budget-led.

In particular, the development project showed that attempts at involvement are likely to succeed if they engage people's concerns, and if they are clearly focused so that both the purpose of the process and its limits are clearly visible from the start. Moreover, our work with practitioners also showed the advantages of a focused approach to skills analysis and development which starts with 'where practitioners are at', rather than where policy makers and senior management would like them to be.

Looking back, it now seems as if one thing which the project showed was that service users, carers and practitioners can come together by focusing on shared objectives, even if their starting points are very different, provided that the pace of the work is not forced and people feel able to develop their own ideas in their own ways. This is an important point which anyone starting a collaborative piece of work ought to bear in mind.

The project was also collaborative in another sense. It could be seen as a collaborative form of communication which enabled people first to identify and then to discuss key issues with one another. We learnt that people benefited from being facilitated to develop their ideas; that they needed opportunities to engage with one another and form relationships; and that they needed time to explore and then to consolidate new information. We acknowledge that none of these things may be very new or surprising, but they are nonetheless vital to the success of any collaborative endeavour.

Collaboration – the culture

Because of the way in which it drew all the different threads of the project together, the get-together meeting provided us with an insight into some of the defining characteristics of what we have described as collaboration culture.

In many ways the culture concept emerging from the workshop was one which had echoes of ideas which emerged earlier on in the project. In particular, it evoked the image of the 'web of cooperation and communication' described by some of the nurses and social workers at an earlier stage. But it was more focused and systematic.

Collaboration is a way of working with other people which is characterized by the following basic assumptions:

- Effective communication is never to be taken for granted. It requires a constant investment of time, energy and thought. This includes spending time listening to and talking to other people, rather than simply making assumptions about them, and it also involves a willingness to think critically about underlying patterns and styles of communication.
- Relationships are valued. This means treating people with respect, being prepared to work at developing trust and recognizing that supporting other people or gaining support for yourself is an integral part of professional work in the field of community care. This is linked to another assumption which is that a strong set of collaborative relationships can deal with conflict in an open and constructive way and may even be further strengthened by the experience.
- Empowerment is an integral part of community care practice. In collaboration culture, all actions are constantly scrutinized for their impact on the position of service users in relation to other members of collaborative networks, and in relation to the power over their lives all too often still wielded by welfare bureaucracies of all kinds in both the state and the independent sector.
- Processes of assessment and planning are shared, open and flexible. This involves a commitment to creativity and a willingness to involve people widely, both in relation to the identification of needs and the accessing of appropriate resources.

- Actively working together with others involves a commitment to shared objectives. This also implies acknowledging responsibilities to others as well as having expectations of them.
- The search for quality is a never-ending one. There will be processes by which both outcomes and ways of working are constantly reviewed, and processes of review will be open to service users, carers and others with whom practitioners are working.

Constructing the web

Rather than divide collaboration culture rather arbitrarily into knowledge, values and skills, we have taken the view that it is better to approach it as an integrated whole but to recognize that there are specific skills which may be required to build it. The concept of collaboration as a 'web of communication and cooperation' also suggests a new way of thinking about skills – one linked to the process of constructing the web.

The development project convinced us that, like any other body of skills, collaborative work can be practised at a variety of levels from the most basic to the most complex. This in turn has led us to focus first on some of the basic skills of collaboration.

What follows can be read in two ways. It can be seen as outlining what amounts to a set of guidelines for newly qualified workers. Or alternatively, it can be used as a checklist for more experienced workers who want to ensure that attention has been paid to the basics in any collaborative work they are currently undertaking.

We make this distinction between the full range of collaborative skills and what we describe as collaborative basics partly because this was the distinction made by those who participated in the workshop. It came over particularly strongly from our discussions with service users, for example. But we also make it because it seems to fit in with how we actually learn: not all at once, but gradually and continuously.

Learning about learning

In thinking about the process of skill development, we inevitably have to think about learning itself. If human evolution teaches us anything, it is that our success as a species is in large part due to our ability to learn from our experience and to apply this learning in ways which generate new and different kinds of experiences for ourselves and others. This interaction between experience, thought and practice lies at the heart of our humanity

and yet it has taken our formal educational systems a long time to recognize the essentially interactional nature of the learning process, a process in which thought, action and reflection are intertwined in a continuous spiral.
  The implications seem to be that:

- Learning about collaboration is likely to be a continuous process and one that nourishes itself, for over a period of time ideas are developed and their consequences experienced, in turn laying the foundation for further learning.
- This process of reflecting on experience, giving it meaning and applying the resulting insights to collaborative practice, requires a shift from a rational scientific model based on seeking to control learning processes to something much more experiential.
- Learning from collaborative experiences is, in large part, dependent on a process of attending to and learning from those you collaborate with: a process which is likely to be educational for them as well.

Putting all these points together, it is not too far-fetched to describe learning about collaboration as rather like the process of learning a new language and, as with any new language, we need to start with the basics.

Collaborative credibility

All those who have qualified as professionals nevertheless still need to demonstrate what the Central Council for Education and Training in Social Work refer to as 'professional credibility' (Central Council for Education and Training in Social Work, 1990, s.3.5.i). We found in the development project that basic qualities, such as honesty, reliability and an up-to-date knowledge of resources, are valued very highly by the users of services. But we also found that simply possessing a professional qualification was no guarantee of this kind of professional credibility. Moreover, a similar emphasis on honesty, reliability and knowing what one is talking about came over very strongly from the practitioners in the project.
  These elements of collaborative credibility are not enough in themselves to make collaboration work, but the evidence from the development project was that without them the process of developing a collaborative relationship will not even get to square one. It should also be emphasized that practitioners need to demonstrate not only that they can be trusted, but that they have the ability to communicate qualities of honesty, reliability and knowledgeability to service users, carers and other practitioners alike. This is a skilled activity which cannot be learnt or demonstrated overnight. It

will inevitably take time, and with any new relationship it will have to be demonstrated all over again.

Anti-oppressive values

The project showed clearly the importance attached to certain key values by all those who participated in it. Broadly speaking these values could be summed up as a commitment to anti-discriminatory practice on the one hand and empowerment on the other. Professionals, service users and carers all agreed that they expected the nurses, social workers and others with whom they had dealings to be committed to the fight against injustice. There was a feeling among all those who participated in the project that even newly qualified professionals should be able to show that they are aware of injustice and willing to do what they can to oppose it. Although some skills might be missing, all agreed that the key values should be in place.

As with credibility, a commitment to anti-discriminatory practice is something that all those involved in collaborative work need to be able to communicate effectively to others. In other words, one of the preconditions of collaboration is that it is not enough to be committed to anti-racism, anti-sexism, or any other 'ism'. This commitment needs to be demonstrated to others in an active way. Even experienced workers need to remember that there is a continuing need for this in the way that they conduct their relationships and respond to issues. These are the kind of commitments that can never and should never be taken for granted.

A basic understanding of the importance of empowerment and a willingness to act on this understanding are vital components of collaboration which must, if it is to have any meaning, involve sharing power. While newly qualified workers might not be expected to be able to undertake some forms of empowerment, all those involved agreed that it was a fundamental expectation that anyone seeking to form a collaborative working relationship should demonstrate a willingness to share power and on occasion to accept constructive criticism.

Teaching and learning about the basics

Line managers, training sections and trainers could adopt a number of the strategies listed below. If they do not, practitioners can make use of this list themselves to make what seem to us to be some very reasonable demands:

- All newly qualified community care practitioners should receive a balanced workload which enables them to tackle the relevant issues; and more experienced workers should continue to have the time to reflect on their practice and the encouragement needed to ensure that both collaborative credibility and anti-oppressive values remain fresh and creative elements of practice rather than simply becoming rather tired bits of rhetoric.
- Expectations of newly qualified staff should be pitched at a realistic level. It needs to be recognized that it is just as unreasonable to expect a newly qualified worker to make key decisions on their own about risks to adults as it is about risks to children. But it is also unwise to put even experienced practitioners constantly in the position of having to balance collaborative principles against risk factors without giving them the opportunity to refresh their collaborative practices in less demanding situations.
- Adequate opportunities for supervision must exist so that new professionals are able to engage in a process of recognizing and consolidating their competencies, and more experienced practitioners are enabled to continue to learn by being able to share uncertainties and vulnerabilities.
- Opportunities should be created for peer group support and discussion (equally useful for both newly qualified practitioners and those who are more experienced).
- Specific training on anti-discriminatory practice, user and carer involvement and working with value conflicts should be available to all groups of workers. In relation to user involvement, it would be especially helpful to make use of service user trainers both on conventional courses and as an alternative to them.

Training and resources for service users and carers

While it is important to make appropriate use of service users and carers as trainers, it is also important to recognize that they may have training needs as well.

Collaboration needs to come from both sides of the welfare counter. Service users and carers need opportunities to develop skills to work with community care services as individuals and organizations, just as community care practitioners need to develop skills to work with them. This study highlighted the training needs of users and carers and their organizations as well as those of practitioners. This needs to be acknowledged in education and training for practitioners. There needs to be recognition developed in professional training for collaboration that service users and carers will themselves need training and resources.

Are you ready to move on?

Evaluating whether you or someone you supervise is ready to move on to more advanced collaborative work, or whether there is a need for further consolidation around the basics, is not an easy or straightforward matter. To help make this slightly less complicated we have made use of the findings from the project to develop a tool which should help to act as a starting point.

It is a *self-evaluation schedule* which is mainly designed for use by the individual practitioner, but it can be used by managers or supervisors or by peer groups. It may also be helpful to service users and carers, and their organizations, who want to evaluate and improve the practice they experience.

For those wishing to develop their skills in collaborative work further, a number of new challenges present themselves. We explore these in the next chapter.

Summary

In this chapter we have tried to 'unpack' some of the broad issues raised by the project. We began by acknowledging the way the process in which we were engaged mirrored its subject matter. We then moved on to explore some of the key features of collaboration culture, especially collaborative forms of communication, relationship building, empowerment, assessment and working with other people. Finally we looked at some of those things which we called collaborative 'basics' – that mixture of collaborative credibility and anti-oppressive values and attitudes which forms the bedrock of collaborative practice.

Exercise

Basic Skills in Collaborative Work

A self-evaluation schedule

This is not a test. It is a tool for self-evaluation. It is therefore best seen as a way for you to understand your own levels of skill better and to help you to identify staff development targets for yourself.

1   Have you demonstrated 'collaborative credibility' by:

a)   consistently doing what you say you will do or if unable to do so by explaining why?

Evidence: . . . .

b)   engaging in frank and open discussion with those with whom you are collaborating – especially service users and carers – about uncomfortable, difficult or painful issues?

Evidence: . . . .

c)   having up-to-date knowledge about benefits, legislation and services and the ability to make constructive use of this knowledge?

Evidence: . . . .

d)   showing a willingness to listen to others and to take notice of what they say in all areas of your work including assessment?

Evidence: . . . .

2   Have you consistently challenged discriminatory attitudes and poli-cies when needed and thought critically about your attitudes and actions:

a)   in direct work with service users and carers?

Evidence: . . . .

b)   with your colleagues?

Evidence: . . . .

c)   with other practitioners / agencies?

Evidence: . . . .

3   Have you sought consistently to empower others by:

a)   finding ways to share power with service users and carers?

Evidence: . . . .

b)   challenging policies and practices which prevent service users and carers making their voices heard?

Evidence: . . . .

4   Have you been able to work with value conflicts by:

a)   helping all those involved to understand the nature and depth of the value conflict?

Evidence: . . . .

b)   taking account of actual and potential value conflicts in the process of negotiating and planning with service users, carers or other practitioners?

Evidence: . . . .

9 The skills

Building a collaboration culture

As we saw in the last chapter, the development project helped all those involved to see that there were certain basic principles involved in laying the groundwork for what we have called collaboration culture. Getting the basics right is as important in collaborative work as in anything else and, as we also saw in the last chapter, this is in itself a skilled activity. But the project also showed that a fully fledged collaboration culture requires more than this. It involves:

- Building interpersonal collaborative networks.
- Building inter-organizational and intra-organizational collaborative networks.

Through these activities the key themes of collaboration culture are given substance and meaning.

The interpersonal sphere consists of all those collaborative practices which are concerned with linking between service users, carers and other practitioners in order to develop a collective response to individual rights and needs. For those working with service users and carers on a face-to-face level, whether they are nurses, social workers or occupational therapists, this is inevitably the sphere of collaborative practice with which they are mostly preoccupied.

In contrast, although the inter-organizational and intra-organizational spheres are also concerned to some extent with relationships between individuals, here individuals relate to one another as representatives of groups, services or agencies. Linking is not just between individuals across organizational boundaries but between groups, services and organizations of all kinds in order to improve ways of collectively identifying and responding to community needs. The emphasis is on developing new networked structures, systems and cultures. Community care practitioners may well get involved to some extent in this type of work in relation to service innovation. But for service managers, community care planners, commissioners and those concerned with encouraging and supporting independent service users' and carers' organizations, this type of work is likely to be a major preoccupation.

In what follows, we explore the key skills needed for building a culture of collaboration and locate them in the context of a range of interpersonal and inter / intra-organizational practices. Each area of collaborative skill is linked to a set of exercises to help make the discussion less abstract and to enable practitioners to test out or further develop their own collaborative skills.

Skills in collaborative communication

Improving the quality and flow of communication

We learnt that when working with individual service users, a whole range of practices can help to improve the general quality of communication and ensure that the right information gets to the right people. These practices include network conferences; regular meetings with service users, citizen advocates and carers; long-term inter-agency liaison; following up written contacts with telephone calls; identifying a core group of named individuals as key workers, and so on. But it is important that thought is given to the appropriateness of whatever is done.

This means that part of the skill lies in the analysis of communication problems as well as the possession of a repertoire of possible solutions to those problems. This takes us back to one of the basic issues dealt with in the last chapter, that of attending to what other people are saying. In itself, it is not enough, but without it analysis is impossible.

The project clarified the point that at an inter / intra-organizational level there is a need to think more strategically about both the flow and the quality of communication. Strategic options include newsletters, inter-agency meetings, and meetings with service users' and carers' groups and organizations. But as with interpersonal communication, the response needs to be an appropriate one. Therefore an ability to attend to what others are saying and to analyse the nature of communication problems is essential.

Ensuring all voices are heard

One issue emerging clearly from the project was that good communication does not consist solely of finding ways to ensure that those who already have a voice can speak more clearly to one another. It is also a matter of enabling those who have previously been ignored or silenced to find a voice and to ensure that others pay attention to it. Good communication is empowering because it creates new opportunities both to speak and to listen. A key skill lies therefore in exploring and then developing new kinds of communication opportunities for those who have previously been silent.

The project emphasized that enabling small organizations and community groups to be heard involves linking communication systems to participatory objectives. In particular it means paying attention to feedback processes at every stage of the decision-making process.

A key skill for practitioners and managers is therefore being able to make involvement an empowering rather than an oppressive practice by ensuring that concepts of effective user involvement and accountability to the community are built into participatory arrangements. This can be done either directly or through lobbying, another skilled activity.

Whatever they do, practitioners and managers need constantly to bear in mind the empowering potential of new opportunities for communication.

Reducing conflict through effective communication

While real conflicts of view – between practitioners and carers, for example – cannot simply be wished away, the project seemed to indicate that when opportunities were created for sharing not just opinions and decisions, but the thinking lying behind them, then it was sometimes possible to reduce conflict and develop a shared understanding. The skills involved here include overcoming one's own feelings and motivating others to overcome theirs sufficiently to begin a process of sharing either on a one-to-one basis or in a group.

At an inter / intra-organizational level one of the key skills is to reduce the potential for confusion and conflict through the use of specific models of communication. Frequently, locating responsibility in named individuals and ensuring everyone knows who these individuals are will be all that is needed. Sometimes, however, it will not be enough for these individuals to be positive and purposeful. Where an agency is about to take on new responsibilities or to give up old ones, opportunities for discussing all the implications openly and honestly may mean investing time in developing more widespread forums for face-to-face discussion between opposite numbers, preferably at a number of different organizational levels, from that of senior management to that of the practitioner.

Exercise

Putting communication skills into collaborative practice

1   **Identify a situation in which you are involved with other practitioners / service users / carers and in which you feel either or both the quality of communication and the flow of information could be improved. Try to answer the following questions:**

How does the present system work? What are its advantages and disadvantages?

How might the quality of information flowing around this network be improved and what might be achieved as a result of any improvement?

2   **Identify any individuals or groups who tend to miss out on important information.**

How might the system of communication be changed in order to include rather than exclude them?

Outline the steps you would take to achieve some or all of these changes.

3   **Identify a situation in which you are involved with other practitioners / service users / carers and in which you feel that some powerful individuals or groups dominate all discussions at the expense of others who are less powerful.**

What are the barriers to participation in the communication network? How might they be overcome?

How might you go about supporting those who are silent to develop a voice?

How might you go about ensuring that others listen to and take note of these new voices?

4   **Identify a situation in which you are involved with other practitioners / service users / carers and in which conflict is linked to poor communication.**

How might misunderstandings be rectified?

How might you enable conflicting points of view to be heard?

How might the communication system be used to acknowledge and contain conflict rather than to deny and amplify it?

> **5 Identify a situation in which you are involved with other practitioners / service users / carers and in which inappropriate language or style of communication is being used.**
>
> What is it that is inappropriate?
>
> How might you set about trying to ensure that a more appropriate kind of language is used?

Skills in the use of appropriate language

This could take many different forms, most obviously using an interpreter when there is no common language, but also including forms of direct communication sensitive to the needs of children; open-ended styles of questioning when exploring needs with service users and carers; and knowledgeable but flexible ways of discussing issues with other practitioners. Sometimes the need might simply be to avoid using oppressive jargon. The skills involved here include an ability to analyse situations in terms of dominant linguistic features, which goes beyond the question of whether someone speaks English or not. It also includes an ability to be aware of one's own language and to modify it as appropriate. As with many other communications skills, an ability to use language appropriately is at root an empowering strategy.

Similar issues arise at an inter / intra-organizational level. For example, publishing leaflets in a variety of languages is essential; and when chairing meetings it is important to ensure that if service users and carers are present, language styles include rather than exclude those who are unfamiliar with professional jargon. Although the context might be different, the skills involved are closely related to those already identified for interpersonal work.

Skills in relationship work

All collaborative networks are *social* networks. Whether they consist of individuals or organizations, the effectiveness of communication and levels of cooperation will depend on the extent to which all those involved are able to build and manage their relationships successfully.

Handling conflict

The project made it clear that an ability to analyse and manage ambivalence and conflict and its impact on oneself was an important aspect of the process of developing and sustaining community care networks. A key skill seems to be finding ways of making it safe to expose the sources of conflict and discuss them. This does not always resolve conflict but does seem to reduce the destructive power of conflict-laden issues by demonstrating confidence in the strength of relationships.

Confronting discrimination

Serious dilemmas can be posed when one or more of those with whom one is seeking to collaborate demonstrates discriminatory attitudes or behaviour. Sometimes it may be necessary to terminate the collaboration, but during the course of the project we also heard about ways of challenging this kind of behaviour. The critical element here seems to be a collaborative network able collectively to demonstrate its disapproval and having the power to enforce a change in behaviour. A key skill therefore consists of ensuring that anti-discriminatory values are built into the basic assumptions underpinning the collaboration and having the confidence to mobilize support on the basis of these values so that any discriminatory behaviour will be immediately challenged if it appears.

Institutionalized discrimination may be more appropriately addressed at an inter / intra-agency level. Often the problem can be seen as one of lack of responsiveness or accountability, often associated with a lack of any real relationship to certain parts of the community. In the case of a culturally insensitive meals-on-wheels service, for example, involving organizers in direct discussions with service users, friends and relatives and enabling them to access advice about easy-to-prepare recipes might play a part in a successful anti-discriminatory strategy oriented towards changing the relationship between meals-on-wheels and the community.

Developing trust

One of the issues that emerged very strongly from the project was the importance of building and sustaining trust, mutual respect and mutual understanding between the members of a support network. Skills involved here include being able to encourage informal contact between members of the support network, facilitate group discussions, explore opportunities for mutual aid and support and promote joint visits.

At an inter / intra-organizational level, trust also involves planned and regular interaction with opportunities for the kind of collective action which

Exercise

Putting relationship skills into collaborative practice

1 **Think of a situation in the past where you were trying to work with someone from another agency or a service user or carer and relationships deteriorated because of unresolved conflict.**

If you had the chance to go back to that situation now what might you do differently that would enable the conflict to be addressed in a constructive way?

2 **Suppose that another professional with whom you were working closely as part of a collaborative network made a racist, sexist or disablist remark about a service user.**

What would you do?

Would you act alone or with others? If the latter, with whom?

What would be the impact of your response on network relationships?

3 **In the course of your work, you are about to embark on a new set of relationships with other practitioners, service users and carers.**

What would help to build trust between all these people?

What would you do first to facilitate this process?

4 **Imagine that you yourself needed additional support in your professional role.**

What would you be likely to need support with?

How would you go about identifying potential supporters?

Would you need the help of one or more 'brokers' – if so who?

How would you make contact or, if using a broker, how would the broker do it?

What might best motivate your potential supporters to respond to your needs?

If successful in recruiting supporters, what kind of obligations might you have to them in the future?

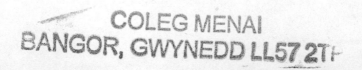

leads agencies to develop confidence in one another and the strength of their relationships.

Developing support

The ability to develop personal support networks is a key aspect of collaborative work. This involves all members of a collaborative network either being able directly to meet one another's needs or alternatively helping to ensure that some needs are met in other ways.

Support can mean different things to different people and what is supportive in one situation may not be so in another. But whether support is emotional, practical, oriented to sharing or oriented to campaigning, consideration needs to be given to ways of identifying and recruiting potential supporters. The skills involved include being able to identify sources and patterns of potential as well as actual support, forging links with key figures able to broker support and being able to apply these principles to one's own needs as well as those of others.

It is not usual to think of support at an inter-agency level but it is possible for small voluntary or service users' organizations to be quite isolated and vulnerable when working alongside larger, much more powerful and more effectively resourced organizations, such as social services departments. In these situations finding ways of channelling additional resources to small organizations can be very supportive. This can take the form of making knowledge and expertise available as well as money. The skills involved here are similar to those employed in evaluating more personal support needs. But there is a need to understand that different kinds of organizations may have different kinds of needs.

The best way of exploring what is meant by competency in the mobilization of support is to think what it might imply if you were to attempt to recruit additional support for yourself.

Skills in empowerment

Advocacy

One of the findings from the project was the importance attached to a willingness and an ability to speak up for service users and carers in a credible and effective way. The skills involved include being able to present well-prepared, well-argued and comprehensive assessments which link community care needs to the rights of individuals to exercise choice and control over their own lives (see Skills in assessment and planning, p. 143). But they go wider than this, as well.

At an inter / intra-agency level, an ability to lobby for changes in the way in which health and social services are planned and delivered so as to pay more attention to the question of 'rights' was widely seen as a key advocacy skill and one which would make the notion of 'user-led' services more meaningful than it sometimes is.

Involving service users and carers in defining and assuring quality

Individual service users may have been given formal rights to complain, but the project showed that they often sought a more active role in relation to service quality. For care managers, in particular, it was clear that safeguarding quality meant working with service users and carers to develop 'care packages' which reflected a real concern with quality of life as well as quality of care in a traditional sense. This, in turn, meant that it was important to maintain an active concern with rights and choices, as well as perceived dependency needs. The skills involved include having the ability to work together with service users and carers to develop creative and life-enhancing plans for support, and to challenge service providers who continue to approach their task on the basis of a lowest common denominator service.

At an inter / intra-organizational level the project showed that there were still too few opportunities for service users, carers and their organizations or other community groups to make an impact on the increasingly important processes by which quality standards were defined and quality assurance systems implemented. Key skills therefore include the ability to support service users and carers to develop their own priorities in discussion with one another and to have regular and reliable opportunities to communicate with community care agencies about these priorities. In these ways involvement becomes an integral part of the whole quality system rather than a tokenistic afterthought.

Promoting responsiveness

At an interpersonal level this focuses on ensuring that all those involved in supporting individuals are prepared to respond positively to the needs and wishes of service users and carers. It involves having the skill to challenge other practitioners who seem to be unreasonably rigid in their approach. But it also involves being able to enable other practitioners to explore ways in which they might overcome real obstacles to their responsiveness, including bureaucratic and resource constraints.

At a broader, inter-organizational level, structural constraints on responsiveness need to be challenged. This involves being able to act as a cultural innovator promoting new organizational values. Pursuing this within one's own organization may be important but it is unlikely to be enough. Service users need to be assured that all the agencies they deal with share the same kind of values in relation to responsiveness. So there is a need to be able to deploy these skills in the context of inter-organizational forums. To be

---

Exercise

Putting empowerment skills into collaborative practice

1   Assuming that in your workplace opportunities for advocacy arise quite frequently:

Are there any opportunities for advocacy which you think you might have missed recently?

Why might opportunities for advocacy be missed in this way?

Think of ways in which advocacy might be undertaken without disempowering service users.

2   Assuming that you have some responsibilities in relation to quality assurance in your organization:

How might service users be involved more thoroughly than at present in setting and monitoring service standards?

What issues might need to be addressed to ensure that this happens?

3   In what ways could your organization be made more flexible and responsive to the needs and wishes of service users and carers?

What problems might need to be overcome first?

How would you set about tackling these problems bearing in mind your position within your organization?

4   Thinking of the individual service users or service users' groups that you have contact with:

How might you go about discovering their training needs?

How might the use of service user trainers become an integral part of staff development?

successful in this, practitioners, including managers, will need to have the skill to develop alliances with service users' and carers' organizations.

Facilitating training for service users and carers

The project demonstrated there is an unmet need for training among service users and carers. At an interpersonal level this may mean simply being willing and knowing how to share community care knowledge and skills with others, especially service users and carers. Sharing skills helps to demystify professionalism and to give service users and carers more sense of involvement and control. It is a reciprocal process. So practitioners may stand to learn something new as well! It may also mean helping service users and carers to contact one another so as to form 'action learning sets' or groups which enable knowledge and skills to be shared and developed.

At an inter-organizational level, the issues and therefore the skills are more likely to focus on finding ways of channelling resources to service users' and carers' groups and creating new learning opportunities for them.

Skills in assessment and planning

Engagement

The project confirmed the truth of the traditional wisdom that effective assessment and planning depends on an ability to engage with other people. But in the context of community care this means that assessors have to have the ability to empathize with and relate to a very wide range of people without losing their primary concern with the needs of the service user.

At the level of inter-agency planning / commissioning / purchasing, engagement is equally important. All the key stakeholders, including service users' and carers' organizations, have to feel an integral part of the process. If they feel marginalized or excluded, any plans that emerge will suffer from a lack of support and commitment. Engaging with organizations at this level means paying real attention to their views and acknowledging that a certain level of conflict is likely to occur without allowing this to inhibit the development of relationships.

Needs, risks and opportunities

The project showed that a collaborative approach to community care involves a shift away from a traditional concept of assessment, often dominated by concepts of risk, towards one in which the creation of new *opportu-*

nilies for improving the quality of life is a central objective and the characteristic process is one of continuous dialogue with service users, carers and other practitioners.

The skills involved in opportunity assessment and opportunity planning include an ability to collaborate with others and especially service users in analysing both existing patterns of interaction and evaluating the potential of new forms of life-enhancing support. This again reinforces the critical importance of an ability to attend to what other people are saying.

At a wider level, the shift from a concept of risk to a concept of opportunity has radical implications for community care planning. It involves focusing not on certain standardized notions of need and their relationship to existing services, but on the kind of opportunities which would improve the overall level of support and quality of life of individuals and groups drawn from a diverse set of local cultures and family structures. At the same time, profiling services will have to give way to auditing community resources in a much more flexible and creative way. The skills involved in this would have to include the ability to engage with and take notice of a wide range of service users', carers' and other groups, alongside powerful vested interests, such as social services departments and health authorities and representatives of the emerging independent sector.

Awareness of multiple perspectives

It is inevitable that any system which involves talking to service users, carers or other practitioners will generate a situation in which individual assessors will have to take account of multiple perspectives. The key skills here are concerned with enabling people to express their views and then deciding not that some are right and others are wrong, but that they will all embody some part of the truth of the situation. This will enable conflicts of view to be handled sensitively.

If the aim is to develop an inter-organizational rather than a purely interpersonal collaboration, then this issue takes on a new kind of meaning. It is a question of understanding that building a concept of need at this broader level cannot be separated from the aims and objectives of different organizations and how these relate to the interests of various groupings across the whole field of community care. Concepts of 'community need', therefore, need to be sensitive to the politics of community care.

Creativity

Almost by definition, the concept of opportunity planning requires creativity. At a time when guidelines and detailed procedures of one kind or another are threatening to reduce human services to a series of mechanical tasks, to talk about creativity may seem hopelessly out of touch with reality. But we would argue that the whole concept of a needs-led service is meaningless if imagination and innovation are not placed at the centre of community care practice. Some might argue that it is almost a contradiction in terms to talk about skills in creativity but it is clear that an ability to respond to the demands of a situation in a fresh way, untrammelled by what sometimes passes for traditional wisdom, will be of great importance. It also needs to be recognized that opening up fuller and more open-ended discussions with service users and carers will enable them to be creative in their thinking as well. This will in turn reinforce the creativity of assessors.

At an inter / intra-agency level, creativity is also important. After all, although it will be possible to learn from what has been done elsewhere, specific issues thrown up by a particular client group, a particular locality

---

Exercise

Putting assessment and planning skills into collaborative practice

1   Whether you are a purchaser or a provider you are likely to be concerned with some aspects of assessment and planning.

How might you start to involve a broad range of people in a collaborative approach to the assessment task?

How might this process be made manageable and service users assured that their needs, rights and wishes remain uppermost in your mind?

2   Traditional assessments often focus on the question of risk.

How might you ensure that in future your own assessments or those undertaken by others give more weight to opportunities for life enhancement?

3   How might a number of very different views about needs contribute to an integrated assessment? How might you go about setting up a process which could achieve this?

4   Under pressure of work it is often difficult to be imaginative in relation to assessment and planning.

As an exercise try to think of five different ways in which the same set of individual or community needs could be met. To make this more interesting you might like to limit the contribution of standard services to a minor role in four out of the five!

or a particular blend of local groups and agencies, in principle add up to both a need and a recipe for innovative thinking.

Skills in collaborative working

Clarifying goals, roles and tasks

Almost all collaborative working arrangements have to overcome a series of hurdles before they can begin to be effective. The development project showed that misunderstandings and false conceptions of one another's roles are commonplace. It is therefore essential for the success of any collaborative venture that attention is given at the outset to clarifying goals, roles and tasks. This should not be seen as a once and for all event, but something which is constantly reviewed. Sometimes it may be useful to formalize this understanding as it exists at any one time and commit it to writing. But it is important that clarity does not lead to rigidity or demarcation disputes. The purpose of clarifying key collaborative issues is not to produce a set of job descriptions. Rather, it is to develop a set of shared basic assumptions around which the collaboration can grow organically. The skills involved in this include an ability to think in a task-oriented way, and to combine maximum flexibility about who does what with maximum clarity about any decisions made.

Contracts are often useful ways of enabling those who intend working together to clarify the terms of their relationships. Inter-organizational work is no exception. Increasingly, purchasers, providers, service users and carers will need to come together around shared understandings about the range of support services that could be available to care managers. Working towards legally binding contracts should not mean that broader issues are lost sight of. It is important that people are not rushed into commitments before they feel ready. There is a skill involved in facilitating an open-ended phase of exploration of possibilities as well as a skill in judging the best moment to conclude negotiations and sign a contract.

Handling multiple accountability

Multi-disciplinary and inter-agency collaboration, and collaboration between professionals and service users and carers, all raise questions of accountability.

The project helped everyone involved to see that agreements about accountability must be made meaningful to all those involved. In particular, service users, carers and other community care practitioners need to be aware of what kinds of rights they have to information, consultation and participation in decision making. There are skills involved in translating notions of multiple accountability from the rhetorical to the practice dimension, by paying close attention to the needs and sometimes conflicting interests of all those involved and being able to work together to develop the system of accountability.

At an inter-organizational level, community care will not work unless attempts are made to thrash out issues of confidentiality, professional autonomy, line management responsibilities, the purchaser/provider split and service user involvement in such a way as to provide a useful framework of accountability for practitioners. The skills involved here will include an ability to negotiate between the competing claims of particular notions of accountability.

Coordination

Collaboration is intimately connected with coordination. At the level of the care package, the framework for coordination is laid by early negotiations about roles, goals and tasks. But while this might set the overall strategy, there is still a need for day-to-day coordination, if only to ensure that small problems do not become large ones and any conflicts are dealt with at an early stage.

Having said this, there is a tension between the concept of authority inherent in the notion of coordination and the participative principles of collaboration. Care managers and others will need to be able to find ways of managing this tension. Sometimes this might be done by enabling service users themselves to act as coordinators. But even if this is not the case, coordinators need to have the ability to give some tangible expression to the principle that the power of collaborative coordination is derived entirely from the collaborative network itself and its collective wish to accomplish its tasks effectively.

Similar issues arise at a broader level. It may be difficult for various groups and agencies to collaborate effectively unless one agency or group takes on responsibility for coordinating the multi-agency effort. Those taking on roles like this as representatives of their organizations will need to have skills in chairing meetings and, from time to time if conflict emerges, skills as conciliators as well.

The question of power and accountability may in some ways be more easily resolved at this level, but there will still be a need for skills in clarifying the extent to which the coordinator is simply acting for the collaborative network as a whole rather than in his or her own right. Moreover, while coordinators can reduce democracy, they can also enhance it. It is the larger, more powerful agencies which may feel most constrained, and

Exercise

Putting skills in collaborative working into collaborative practice

1   In your day-to-day collaborative work:

What kind of issues cause the most confusion and what could be done to prevent this kind of confusion arising in the future?

What might be the advantages and disadvantages associated with a written contract?

2   Negotiation is a process. It can be divided into three stages: exploration, discussion and decision making.

How would you apply this model to your own work?

3   Identify a situation in which you are working with more than one other person. Divide a sheet of paper into as many columns as there are individuals or groups involved in the collaborative network.

In each column write down the kind of responsibilities that you feel you have to the individuals or groups concerned.

What are the similarities?

What are the differences?

Then write down in each column the kind of responsibilities that you believe these individuals or groups have to you.

What are the similarities?

What are the differences?

What conclusions do you draw about accountability?

4   How might the concept of a network conference be applied to some of the problems of coordination that you currently face?

5   How would you chair a network conference so as to ensure that all those involved felt they were participating in the decision-making process?

the smaller community organizations most empowered, by effective inter-agency coordination.

Skills in review and evaluation

Performance indicators

As already indicated in the earlier discussion about quality assurance, the project emphasized the need for consultation to underpin any attempt to develop yardsticks by which to judge the extent a support network was succeeding in its aims. If there is no consensus on positive or negative indicators, it is very difficult to see how evaluation can take place. This will involve skills in facilitating dialogue on broad issues connected with quality of life objectives, while at the same time focusing attention on the link between these and specific indicators.

At the inter-organizational level it will also be necessary to establish agreements on the expected outcomes of collaboration. Here again it is important that the indicators genuinely reflect the process of meeting needs and not the internal requirements of agencies.

Review processes

Planned review meetings or network conferences in which careful preparation has been made for the involvement of service users and carers as well as practitioners must lie at the base of any process of reviewing the effectiveness of care packages. Being able to set up and facilitate these meetings is a key collaborative skill.

Reviewing inter-agency planning systems also involves skilled facilitation, especially when it comes to giving due weight to the experiences of service users and carers and ensuring that all members of any review committee are fully aware of these experiences.

Monitoring

Concepts of review and evaluation are largely meaningless unless there is a reliable way of monitoring what is going on. This process of monitoring developments needs to involve all those who are in collaboration with one another. At an interpersonal level this may mean that skills are needed to ensure that feedback is continuous and that information is conveyed in a clear and readily understandable form.

At an inter-organizational level, for example when monitoring hospital discharge arrangements, ensuring continuous, clear and accessible feedback may require skills in developing and maintaining appropriate information systems and computer databases. But it will also require skills in opening up these issues to discussion and collective decision making.

Self-criticism

One of the issues which emerged quite strongly from the project was something which is often ignored in discussions about evaluation, and that is the ability to step back and be critical about one's own practice from time to time. Sometimes stubbornness or pride can interfere with the work.

At an interpersonal level this requires an ability to reflect, to consider alternatives and to accept that someone else may be right when you are wrong.

At an inter / intra-organizational level it requires an ability to step beyond the traditional perspectives associated with your own service or agency and to consider changing practices, even if they are well established and all your colleagues feel comfortable with them.

Exercise

Putting review and evaluation skills into collaborative practice

1   Devise a consultation process which would enable you to work with other practitioners, carers and service users to identify some key performance indicators for the community care work in which you are all involved.

2   In your own field of work, what kind of review processes might best express the principles of openness and participation so important to collaborative work while also ensuring an effective outcome?

3   How might you go about planning a monitoring system with other practitioners, carers and service users? How might the views of others influence the kind of information collected and the way it is communicated to others?

4   How might you build opportunities for reflection into your everyday practice, and how might you provide opportunities for others to feed back to you their views about your practice on a regular basis?

Summary

In this chapter we have focused on the pattern of skills associated with collaboration which the project suggests all community care practitioners, regardless of professional background, will need to have or to develop. We have identified skills in communication, relationship work, empowerment, assessment and planning, collaborative working and review and evaluation as critical components of this skills profile and suggested some exercises which could be used to facilitate the process of skill development.

Conclusion

Collaboration – a way of transforming welfare

Throughout this book we believe we have conveyed one message above all others – a simple, but at the same time potentially revolutionary, message. It is that working with other people is not just a different way of delivering traditional welfare services. If taken seriously, it is a way of transforming the nature of welfare systems. This might seem like a far-fetched claim. But the experiences on which this book is based have convinced us that collaboration involves a much deeper and more transformative set of relationships than is usually conveyed by terms such as 'inter-agency work' or 'participation'.

As a result, although this book has been about skills and the process of skill development, it has also been about culture and the process of culture change. We coined the term 'collaboration culture' to draw attention to this and to differentiate our subject matter from that of the all-pervasive 'contract culture' of community care.

As some service users reminded us at an early stage of the development project, the process of developing this new culture is not something that can be postponed. Collaboration is not a luxury. In as complex and interdependent a system as community care has become, collaboration is *essential* if things are not to fall apart.

We began by looking at the collaborative principle in community care and explored its links with a user-driven rather than budget-driven philosophy. We then moved on to the core of the argument, an account of a project concerned with analysing and developing collaborative skills for community care practice, which involved service users, carers, nurses and social workers and which took as its starting point the interrelationship between collaborative skills and collaboration culture.

This entailed finding out more about some of the skills needed for community care practice, while at the same time exploring the overall characteristics of collaborative work and the implications for the future development of community care systems and services.

Key lessons for collaboration

From the project, we drew a number of key lessons about both the new culture and the skills required to build it.

Collaboration needs to permeate community care practices, influencing them at every stage. It is not just a way of organizing service delivery. It is also a way of identifying needs and resources – a 'holistic' or 'open' approach to assessment characterized by multiple perspectives and multiple accountabilities.

Collaborative systems need to be open in another sense as well. They need to be known about and accessible to all sections of the community. This implies a pro-active rather than a reactive form of community care in which being 'close to the community' is a guiding principle.

Thinking collaboratively entails thinking strategically about ways of working with and supporting both individual service users and carers and their local and national groups and organizations. This challenges all concerned to think about the way in which collaboration involves sharing power as well as responsibility.

Collaboration can only exist if negotiation is for real and there is a genuine willingness to adapt roles and relationships to shifting patterns of need.

This raises the question of basic collaborative values. It was made clear to us that collaboration involves a certain kind of value system, characterized by honesty, commitment and reliability. It also involves rediscovering the central significance of the personal dimension in community care. This is not personal in any psycho-pathological sense and we are not arguing for more psychotherapy. Rather the need is to develop and maintain through personal relationships a strong focus on service users' and carers' experiences and the impact of collaboration on the quality of those experiences. This should be the case whether dealing with an individual and his or her problems, or the needs of a whole community.

But all this takes time. Whether building up relationships with service users and carers or with other practitioners, the project showed us we cannot expect results overnight.

One point brought home to us by our work was that it is no use developing a concept of collaboration which is out of tune with reality. The starting point for collaboration has to be a recognition of the scarcity of resources, and it has to be seen as a process of working together both to make the most effective use of those scarce resources and sometimes to challenge the systems by which resources are allocated.

Collaboration culture

Overall, collaboration involves a complex interdependency – a 'web' of communication and cooperation linking community care networks together.

Collaboration culture is what holds this web together. It can be seen in terms of communication processes, relationship issues, empowerment, ways of undertaking assessment and planning, processes of working together and approaches to review and evaluation. But all these form part of a coherent whole and rest upon a foundation of collaborative credibility and anti-oppressive practice.

Individual professionals cannot by themselves be expected to develop collaborative networks. This is demanding work which has to be facilitated by managers. This brings into focus the organizational dimension of collaboration. Collaboration is as much an organizational culture as it is a practitioner culture. It seems that the organizational culture of collaboration is one associated with high levels of autonomy and a facilitative rather than overly controlling style of management. It is clear that some agencies seem to be much further along the road in this than others!

We have identified collaborative skills in relation to the whole spectrum of practice, including communication, relationship work, empowerment, assessment and planning, working together and reviewing and evaluating effectiveness. One distinctive feature of these skills is that they are all closely related to the core of what we have called collaboration culture. As such they could be seen as core collaborative skills.

Another feature of these skills is that they are almost all concerned with the process of developing collaborative networks. This focus on process has been quite deliberate, partly to redress the balance of discussion about skills which seems almost always nowadays to focus narrowly and exclusively on outcomes and partly because everyone agrees that collaboration is desirable, but it is the process of developing collaboration which throws up all the difficult questions concerning change, conflict, identity and role – questions which we felt we needed to address.

A collaborative approach to developing skills

We began the project in the spirit of trying to move away from rigid concepts of skill towards more fluid accounts of practice which link issues, values and ways of doing things together. In our view, skills analysis should not be like butterfly collecting and this is particularly so in the field of community care where innovation is so important and what exists today may not be what exists tomorrow. Now that we are at the end of the project, we feel that what we have had to say about the process of skill development is as important as what we have been able to say about collaborative skills themselves.

We are convinced that collaborative skills can only be developed in a collaborative way. This implies that the process of developing new community care skills and refining old ones should be open and participative rather than closed and didactic. Traditional boundaries between professions and between practitioners and service users need constantly to be questioned, and there needs to be a real commitment both to sharing skills and to taking notice of and learning from others if progress is to be made.

The project had a number of valuable practical outcomes. For example, it led us to try to develop a new form of post-graduate inter-professional education and training in community care. This has in itself been a major collaborative challenge involving negotiation between two different university departments, several professional bodies, a number of local social services departments, some National Health Service trusts and a regional health authority.

But for us, the most important outcome of the project was the creation of a new perspective on collaboration, one that does not separate inter-professional and inter-agency work from work with service users and carers, but sees all these things as connected with one another as part of a collaborative approach to community care practice.

Community care can sometimes feel very complex, confusing and even contradictory. While not wishing to oversimplify or deny the real ethical dilemmas associated with it, we feel we have shown that collaboration can help to clarify as well as confuse; that it has to be a value-driven exercise, not simply an attempt to solve technical puzzles or achieve advantages for one's own agency or profession; and that it opens the door to a new kind of culture from which all those involved in community care may benefit.

Bibliography

Alter, C. and Hage, J. (1993) *Organizations Working Together*, Sage Library of Social Research 191, London: Sage.

Austin, C.D. (1983) 'Case Management in Long-term Care: Options and opportunities', *Health and Social Work*, **8**, no. 1, 16–30.

Baistow, K. (1995) 'Liberation And Regulation: Some paradoxes of empowerment', *Critical Social Policy*, no. 42, Winter, 34–46.

Barnes, C. (1991) *Disabled People In Britain and Discrimination: A case for anti-discrimination legislation*, London: Hurst.

Baxter, C., Poonia, K., Ward, W. and Nadirshaw, Z. (1990) *Double Discrimination: Issues and services for people with learning difficulties from black and ethnic minority communities*, London: King's Fund Centre in conjunction with the Commission for Racial Equality.

Bayley, M.J. (1978) *Community Oriented Systems of Care*, Berkhamstead: The Volunteer Centre.

Begum, N. (1994) 'Optimism, Pessimism and Care Management: The impact of community care policies', in Begum, N., Hill, M. and Stevens, A. (eds), *Reflections: Views of black disabled people on their lives and community care*, CCETSW Paper 32.3, London: CCETSW, 143–59.

Begum, N. and Gillespie-Sells, K. (1994) *Towards Managing User-Led Services*, London: Race Equality Unit.

Benn, S.I. (1982) 'Individuality, Autonomy and Community', in Kamenka, E. (ed.), *Community as a Social Ideal*, London: Edward Arnold.

Beresford, P. (1993) 'Service Users and Networking', in Trevillion, S. (ed.), *Networking and Community Care: An anthropological perspective*, Twickenham: Centre for Comparative Social Work Studies, West London Institute.

Beresford, P. (1994) *Changing the Culture: Involving service users in social work education*, Paper 32.2, London: Central Council for Education and Training in Social Work.

157

Beresford, P. and Croft, S. (1986) *Whose Welfare: Private care or public services?*, Brighton: Lewis Cohen Urban Studies Centre.

Beresford, P. and Croft, S. (1993a) *Community Care and Citizenship*, Workbook 3, Part 1, Community Care, Open University Course, Milton Keynes.

Beresford, P. and Croft, S. (1993b) *Citizen Involvement: A practical guide for change*, London: Macmillan.

British Association of Social Workers (1980) *Clients are Fellow Citizens: Report of the working party on client participation in social work*, Birmingham: BASW.

Campbell, J. (1993) *User's Perspectives*, on Audio-cassette 3, Side 1, Band B, Open University Course K259 Community Care.

Central Council for Education and Training in Social Work (1989) *Requirements and Regulations for the Diploma in Social Work Dip.SW*, London: CCETSW.

Central Council for Education and Training in Social Work (1990) *The Requirements for Post Qualifying Education and Training in the Personal Social Services: A framework for continuing professional development*, Paper 31, London: CCETSW.

Challis, L. (1990) *Organising Public Social Services*, Harlow: Longman.

Cmn 849 (1989) *Caring for People: Community care in the next decade and beyond*, London: HMSO.

Croft, S. and Beresford, P. (1990) *From Paternalism to Participation: Involving people in social services*, London: Open Services Project and Joseph Rowntree Foundation.

Croft, S. and Beresford, P. (1992) 'The Politics of Participation', *Critical Social Policy*, no. 35, Autumn, 20–44.

Department of Health (1993) *Training for the Future: Training and development guidance to support the implementation of the NHS and Community Care Act 1990 and the full range of community care reforms*, London: HMSO.

Department of Health, Social Services Inspectorate (1991) *Training for Community Care: A joint approach*, London: HMSO.

Evans, C. (1994) Co-ordinator, Wiltshire Community Care User Involvement Network, Seeing the Elephant Conference, Devizes, 12 May.

Griffiths, R. (1988) *Community Care: Agenda for action*, London: HMSO.

Gunaratnam, Y. (1992) *Dekhbaal Lai Pukkar/Call for Care*, London: King's Fund Centre in conjunction with the Health Education Authority.

Handy, C.B. (1981) *Understanding Organisations*, Harmondsworth: Penguin.

Hoyes, L. and Means, R. (1993) 'Markets, Contracts and Social Care Services: Prospects and problems', in Bornat, J., Pereira, C., Pilgrim, D. and Williams, F. (eds), *Community Care: A Reader*, London: Macmillan, 287–95.

Hutchinson, A. and Gordon, S. (1992) 'Primary Care Teamwork – Making it a reality', *Journal of Interprofessional Care*, **6**, no. 1, 31–42.

Jones, R.V.H. (1992) 'Teamwork in Primary Care: How much do we know about it?', *Journal of Interprofessional Care*, **6**, no. 1, 25–29.

Keville, H. (1992) 'The Best Qualified Trainers of All', *Care Weekly*, 12 November.

Kuhn, T.S. (1962) *The Structure of Scientific Revolutions*, Chicago: University of Chicago Press.

Le Grand, J. (1990) *Quasi-Markets and Social Policy*, Bristol: School for Advanced Urban Studies.

McCalman, J.A. (1990) *The Forgotten People: Carers in three minority ethnic communities in Southwark*, London: King's Fund Centre.

Morris, J. (1993) *Independent Lives: Community care and disabled people*, London: Macmillan.

Oliver, M. (1990) *The Politics of Disablement*, London: Macmillan.

Oliver, M., Zarb, G., Silver, J., Moore, M. and Sainsbury, V. (1988) *Walking into Darkness*, London: Macmillan.

Payne, M. (1993) *Linkages: Effective networking in social care*, London: Social Care Association Education, Whiting and Birch Ltd.

Peck, E., Ritchie, P. and Smith, H. (1992) *Contracting And Care Management in Community Care: The challenge for local authorities*, Paper 32, London: CCETSW.

Pedison, J. and Sorenson, J.S. (1989) *Organisational Cultures in Theory and Practice*, Aldershot: Avebury.

Peters, T.J. and Waterman, R.H. (1982) *In Search of Excellence: Lessons from America's best-run companies*, New York: Harper Collins.

Rao, N. (1991) *From Providing to Enabling: Local authorities and community care planning*, York: Joseph Rowntree Foundation.

Schein, E.H. (1985) *Organisational Culture and Leadership*, San Francisco: Jossey Bass.

Schon, D.A. (1983) *The Reflective Practitioner: How professionals think in action*, New York: Basic Books.

Shakespeare, T. (1993) 'Disabled People's Self-organisation: A new social movement?', *Disability, Handicap & Society*, **8**, 249–64.

Sharma, T. (1992) 'Patient Voices' *Health Service Journal*, 16 January

Siddiqui, S. (1993) 'More than a Bargain Basement', *Care Weekly*, 4 February.

Smale, G., Tuson, G., Biehal, N. and Marsh, P. (1993) *Empowerment, Assessment, Care Management and the Skilled Worker*, National Institute for Social Work, London: HMSO.

Spratley, J. and Pietroni, M. (1994) *Creative Collaboration: Interprofessional learning priorities in primary health and community care*, London: Marylebone Centre Trust / CCETSW.

Thomas, R.V. and Corney, R.H. (1993) 'Teamwork in Primary Care: The practice nurse perspective', *Journal of Interprofessional Care*, **7**, no. 1, 47–55.

Trevillion, S. (1992) *Caring in the Community: A networking approach to community partnership*, Harlow: Longman.

User Centred Services Group (1993) *Building Bridges: Between people who use and provide services*, London: National Institute for Social Work.

Wagner, G. (1988) *Residential Care: A positive choice*, National Institute for Social Work, London: HMSO.

Walker, A. (1993) 'Community Care Policy: From consensus to conflict', in Bornat, J., Pereira, C., Pilgrim, D. and Williams, F. (eds), *Community Care: A Reader*, London: Macmillan, 204–26.

Index

THE essential SOCIAL WORKER

An introduction to professional practice in the 1990s

THIRD EDITION

MARTIN DAVIES

This third edition has been radically revised and updated and contains an entirely new chapter providing a clear outline of the historical and policy-related framework within which social work operates in areas of particular practice - child care, disability, mental health, old age and criminal justice.

The Essential Social Worker defends the idea of a broadly based profession seeking to maintain disadvantaged people in the community. It bravely confronts the shallowness of many short-term fashions and argues that social work is a uniquely humane contributor to the achievement of welfare in the 1990s and beyond.

A careful reading will ensure that the student gains an understanding of the role of social work in a complex urban society and develops an awareness of the debates which surround it. Social work is often subject to public criticism, but, as the author shows, it has continued to grow in scale and in influence throughout the 20th century, and, although its structure will continue to evolve, social work will remain essential in any society which regards itself as democratic and humane.

Martin Davies is Executive Director of the School of Social Work, University of East Anglia.

1994   240 pages   Hbk   1 85742 100 0   £29.95
Pbk   1 85742 101 9   £12.95

Price subject to change without notification

arena

WORKING TOGETHER IN
Child Protection

An exploration of the multi-disciplinary task and system

MICHAEL MURPHY

This book is a resource for all practitioners, students, managers and trainers who work in the child protection field. It explores the detailed working arrangements of one child protection system and examines the roles and perspectives of the agencies and practitioners who make up that system. It uses examples that are drawn from current practice to outline crucial arguments in the text. It suggests that multi-disciplinary child protection work is both complex and difficult, claiming that a series of structural blockages exist to effective joint working, in particular that we all harbour an ignorance of the perspective and reality of the other agencies and practitioners within the system.

The work goes on to propose a number of measures to be taken by practitioner, agency and government departments that will promote multi-disciplinary working at all levels, suggesting that good multi-disciplinary communication, co-operation and action is synonymous with good child protection work.

The child protection system in England and Wales is used as a case study, but comparisons are drawn with child protection systems in other parts of the world. It is argued that the key concepts and conventions of effective multi-disciplinary child protection work are constant and go beyond the boundaries of single systems.

Michael Murphy is co-ordinator on a Multi-disciplinary Child Protection Resource project.

1995   224 pages   Hbk   1 85742 197 3   £35.00
Pbk   1 85742 198 1   £14.95
Price subject to change without notification

arena

Advocacy

Skills

A HANDBOOK FOR
HUMAN SERVICE PROFESSIONALS

Neil Bateman

Advocacy is a skill used by many people in human service organisations. Social workers, community medical staff and advice workers are a few who will use such skills. Advocacy is used to overcome obstacles and to secure tangible results for customers – extra money, better services and housing. Neil Bateman's book sets out a model for effective professional practice, and outlines a number of approaches to advocacy.

This is a seminal work; no other book has been published in the UK which explains how advocacy skills can be used and developed. Advocacy is becoming part of the everyday work of many people. Advocacy Skills will be a valuable handbook for anyone concerned with the rights of others.

Neil Bateman is currently a Principal Officer with Suffolk County Council, an adviser to the Association of County Councils and a visiting lecturer at the University of East Anglia.

1995   176 pages   1 85742 200 7   £14.95

Price subject to change without notification

arena